THE VOCATIONAL INTERESTS OF
NONPROFESSIONAL MEN

The VOCATIONAL INTERESTS *of* NONPROFESSIONAL MEN

BY

Kenneth E. Clark

University of Minnesota Press, Minneapolis

PUBLISHED IN GREAT BRITAIN, INDIA, AND PAKISTAN BY THE
OXFORD UNIVERSITY PRESS, LONDON, BOMBAY, AND KARACHI
AND IN CANADA BY THOMAS ALLEN, LTD., TORONTO

Foreword

BY JOHN G. DARLEY

"STUDY of interests was initiated in an atmosphere of applied psychology. Most of the worthwhile work has been directed toward the use of interests as a means of solving practical problems. Some 'pure' psychologists should investigate experimentally the nature of interests and how they develop in early life."

This statement appears in the preface to Strong's monumental summary of approximately twenty years of his own research in this area, *Vocational Interests of Men and Women,* published in 1943. Some years later, in 1955, in introducing *Vocational Interest Measurement* to a hardly palpitant audience, I suggested that ". . . those who write of theoretical problems in this area tend to be unfamiliar with the empiric results of vocational interest measurement, and those who present empirical data seem little interested or not adept in theoretical formulations."

In this short volume, Dr. Clark happily combines a sound knowledge of psychometric and statistical theory with a real concern for the empiric problems in interest measurement. As a result, another substantial step has been taken toward our understanding of why men are attracted to different aspects of the many-sided world of work.

This "biography of the Minnesota Vocational Interest Inventory," as its author calls it, is noteworthy in another respect: it is the result of ten years of major research supported by the Office of Naval Research. Admittedly the Navy was concerned with the highly pragmatic problem of classifying its own personnel; to this problem it now has an effective solution. But along with this outcome comes a social gain of major benefit to the civilian economy, for the very standardization of the inventory makes it equally

The Vocational Interests of Nonprofessional Men

applicable to vocational classification, at the skilled trades level, for the large segment of young adults who will not go on to college, but whose contribution to the maintenance and growth of our economy is crucial.

Among the many points of high technical merit in this work, I should like to mention only a few. First, in Chapters 4 and 5 there is an excellent discussion and comparison of the use of criterion-based versus factor-based scoring keys in assessing interests. Second, the nature of the items throughout the inventory stresses the tasks found in the world of work, and the combinations of tasks chosen by the occupational samples contrasted with workers in general give meaning to the occupational labels. Neither gross occupational stereotypes nor personality variables intrude excessively on the derivation of scoring keys. Third, immediate cross-validation samples and varying numbers of scorable items for each occupational key provide evidence of reliability and validity not usually found in test standardization studies. Fourth, Dr. Clark's concluding chapter is an excellent summary, in the light of his own findings, of next research steps in this area of measurement. And finally, this monograph demonstrates that the skilled trades are well above the lower limit of interest differentiation — a point not clear in earlier research, including the pioneering studies of Strong.

This volume does not finish the mapping of the broad terrain of occupational interests and their role in vocational choice, classification, or careers; nor would Dr. Clark make such a claim for his product. But he and his students have charted new ground, have redrawn old landmarks more accurately, and have defined much more clearly the contours of some old problems. Future theorists, as well as future empiricists, will find their travels easier by virtue of this volume, even though difficult and intricate technical issues are raised here.

My gratitude for the privilege of writing this foreword is threefold. I feel honored to add my few words to Dr. Clark's volume, thus continuing our long personal and professional association. I am further delighted that this volume carries forward the dual traditions, at Minnesota, of empiricism as a scientific modality and of concern for the domain of interest measurement. And finally, since writing the foreword meant a careful reading of the manuscript, I appreciate the opportunity of seeing the exciting research findings and new research horizons displayed here.

I commend this volume to the serious consideration of that increasing group of psychologists for whom interest theory and measurement are significant phases in the study of personality development.

Preface

A PROGRAM of research concerned with the measurement of vocational interests cannot be a solitary endeavor, nor can it be of short duration, if it is to deal with the major issues involved in activity preferences as they relate to occupational choice. The work reported in this volume is no exception. It has progressed only because of the generous support of several agencies, the cooperation of large numbers of organized workers and of persons in military service, and the dedicated and inspired assistance of many research workers over a period of years.

A decision to collect meaningful data about the vocational interest patterns of workers at the nonprofessional level involves a decision to commit oneself to a particular research project for many years. The nature of such research requires first the devising of an appropriate instrument, then the administration of this instrument to considerable numbers of workers in various occupations, and finally a great deal of analytical work with the responses obtained. Such research is not possible without substantial financial support. The present report can appear only because the Office of Naval Research has been willing to provide continuous financial support for the research project described herein from the fall of 1946 to the time of this writing. The amount of money involved in the program is not by most standards very large. But the fact that the Office of Naval Research was able to indicate that continuing support would be available made possible the planning of a long-term study which could ultimately arrive at the point in research which this volume reports. The support and interest of several persons in the Office of Naval Research have been sources of encourage-

The Vocational Interests of Nonprofessional Men

ment and pleasure. Drs. John W. MacMillan, John T. Wilson, Howard E. Page, Denzel D. Smith, Glenn L. Bryan, and John Nagay not only have aided in financial matters, but have given invaluable assistance in the collection of data, in obtaining facilities to ease data analysis, and in review and evaluation of the work done. Mr. Sidney Friedman of the Bureau of Naval Personnel and Dr. G. Douglas Mayo of the Naval Air Technical Training Command provided similar support.

The reader should note that no claim is made that this research is completed. Research in the domain of vocational interests must remain openended. It cannot be concluded as long as occupational groups change, as long as stable dimensions of interests remain undetermined, and as long as the total gamut of occupations under scrutiny have not been studied. It has perhaps been characteristic of work done in interest measurement that the likelihood of arriving at a point of closure is rarely suggested. I hope that the reader nonetheless finds in this volume some suggestions for ways in which we can arrive at the point where it no longer is necessary for us to develop an endless series of occupational scales in order fully to describe the motivations for work which characterize young persons about to enter gainful employment.

From 1946 until the end of 1960 the University of Minnesota provided me with substantial free time for continuing this research, and also with the facilities and space which the work required. In addition I was fortunate that the University of Minnesota attracted to its campus an array of able graduate students who participated in this research and to whom much of the credit for the innovations reported in this volume belongs. Major contributions to the research program have been made, somewhat in chronological order, by Mrs. Patricia M. Hayes, Mr. Herbert S. Klapper, Mrs. Carolyn C. White, Mr. Norris Ellertson, Dr. Helen H. Gee, Dr. Dallis K. Perry, Dr. Charles F. Schumacher, Dr. Diane R. Albitz, Dr. Warren T. Norman, and Dr. David P. Campbell. In the preparation of this manuscript Mrs. Martha Hostettler has provided invaluable assistance. In citing these persons it is worthy of note that three times as many as this have participated in some significant role either in the collection of data or in the analysis of the tremendous amount of information with which we have had to deal.

Our analyses have been accomplished in the main by use of punched card and computer equipment. Miss Lois Erickson has provided a substantial amount of support in the handling of the IBM materials; Mr. Rodney

Preface

Larson of the University of Minnesota and Mr. John Olson of the International Business Machines Corporation have given invaluable assistance in using computer facilities for the analysis of our data. If the reader becomes satiated with the number of tables and different sorts of data presented in this volume, he should remember that this is distilled from literally millions of responses which have been utilized in providing the data presented.

The value of research of this sort rests entirely on the quality of the data available. I believe that we were particularly fortunate in obtaining such excellent cooperation from organized labor groups. The St. Paul Trades and Labor Assembly and the Minneapolis Central Labor Union were of great assistance to us in the collection of data. A large number of the skilled trades groups in the Twin Cities of Minneapolis and St. Paul provided us with access to their membership in hopes that this research would improve their ability to recruit the proper type of worker into their trades groups. The chief of Naval personnel, the chief of Naval Air Technical Training, and many other individuals in the military establishment made it possible for us to obtain access to data from Navy enlisted men, from some Air Force groups, and from some Army groups. Some of the work which we did attracted the attention and support of persons in the Veterans Administration in state and local agencies concerned with counseling or rehabilitation, and leaders in various industrial personnel departments and in schools and institutes. The Dunwoody Industrial Institute of Minneapolis made it possible for us to collect data to test the reliability over time of the scales we devised. This willingness to provide us access to their students also made it possible for us to demonstrate that students in various curriculums can be differentiated rather sharply from each other by their scores on a properly devised vocational inventory. The work we were able to do with the Veterans Administration suggests some usefulness for scores of this sort even with hospitalized patients.

The emergence of this volume as a comprehensive report of a long-term research program is possible only because the University of Minnesota, through the University of Minnesota Press, has been willing to underwrite the costs involved. The reader owes great thanks to Miss Jeanne Sinnen of the Press, whose editorial work clarified the presentation throughout. I owe her an even greater debt for her careful and detailed review of the writing, and for her patience and forbearance.

I wish to express my particular gratitude for the advice, encouragement, and insightful analyses which have been provided by Drs. Donald G. Paterson, John G. Darley, E. K. Strong, Jr., and Ralph F. Berdie throughout the period of this research. These men have a richness of background both in interest research itself and in relating interest measurement to other aspects of psychometric work. Through their sage counsels, they have increased the general merit of the procedures employed in the work of this project.

K. E. C.

July 28, 1961

Table of Contents

THE VOCATIONAL INTERESTS OF
NONPROFESSIONAL MEN

✦ 1 ✦

The Measurement of Interests

ALMOST every man has a job. Many find their work fascinating and a source of pride and pleasure. Others escape from work whenever possible and remain at their jobs only because they are paid to do so. Some workers are fortunate enough to have sufficient freedom in a job to accent the parts they like best and to leave for others the tasks they dislike; studies of company executives, for example, reveal the way in which the man influences the nature of the job.

We ordinarily assume that much less freedom exists both in the choice of jobs and in the manipulation of their nature as we move from professional and managerial occupations to skilled trade and sales occupations. And we may sometimes be led to believe that the varieties of preferences expressed by men at professional levels do not exist at nonprofessional levels. Stated in extreme terms, this assumption would hold that professional workers and their peers engage in work that has intrinsic appeal, whereas workers below these levels, especially when far below, tend to labor for wages rather than for love of work.

If such a situation exists, then occupational choice at lower levels becomes more and more a matter of shopping for highest rewards and less and less a searching for work that suits the individual's taste. For occupational counselors, such a view would direct attention to aptitude and ability measures, to work experience, and to the nature of training, and would lead to disuse of measures of vocational interests, activity preferences, and expressed job preferences.

But does this situation exist? The work which this volume reports may

3

shed some needed light. Herein is a description of the development, refinement, and use of an interest inventory with members of certain occupational groups which fall outside the usual definition of professional and managerial occupations. Data on occupational choice are not specifically dealt with, but the findings make a direct contribution to our understanding of occupational choice by studying the characteristics of persons who have found themselves in a given occupational group and have remained there. The work is a pioneering effort since interest measurement has been carried out in the past primarily among those occupations which are normally entered by college students, and in view of the large numbers of persons who are employed in occupations outside this range, the present study is, for this reason if no other, perhaps of considerable import. In addition this volume also reviews work designed to encourage a better understanding of appropriate methods for scoring inventories and work suggesting the most appropriate ways for using such scores.

This study thus reflects one facet of the broad range of activities of American psychologists who have been concerned with the appropriate utilization of the nation's manpower resources. Since World War I, many psychologists have turned to the task of developing testing and classification procedures to use with recruits and officers newly inducted into military service. Others have attended to training problems, job classification, performance rating, or rehabilitation. The problem of increasing the effectiveness of men and women in industrial and educational as well as military settings has engaged the energies of an increasing number of psychologists.

The contributions of these workers have been many and valuable through the development of tests for the identification of talent, through the improvement of school measurement practices in the evaluation of student performance, and through elaborate counseling and guidance programs that help the student get started in the right direction. The emphasis of psychologists upon the need to take into account more than intelligence in the vocational counseling of persons of high ability has had a strong influence on those in charge of selecting candidates for professional and managerial training. Perhaps no group does a better job of screening its potential members than the medical profession, which augments the counseling provided for premedical students in almost every college with a battery of tests and interest measures aimed at weeding out those not likely to do well in medical schools. Life insurance companies, dental schools, graduate departments in many academic areas, public school systems, and many indus-

The Measurement of Interests

trial concerns looking for junior executive trainees all have learned the value of attention to individual differences not only in aptitudes but in interests and personality. While some of the counseling programs, and many of the tests, may have been somewhat oversold, there is a substantial body of information to support the contention that occupational effectiveness at the professional level is increased when persons enter those fields for which they are best fitted, both intellectually and temperamentally.

It is rather surprising to contrast the attention given to assuring effective career selection among college students with that given to the problems of high school students. Almost every college of any repute prides itself on its counseling service, and provides not only professional assistance to students but opportunities for testing a wide variety of personal characteristics. Hardly any high school systems provide comparable service. When counseling is available, the standards are usually much lower than in colleges. In addition, the available instruments for measuring differential characteristics of high school students who waver between various choices of occupations are much less varied and certainly not as fully developed as those used at the college level.

One may argue that the investment in the training of a medical school student is so great that the likelihood of successful completion of the course must be assured by careful screening procedures. From the standpoint of the total society, however, by what standard are we to say that the contentment and effectiveness of a physician are more important than those of a house painter, or a milk wagon driver, or a machinist? There may well be greater national concern about the effectiveness of our 500,000 machinists than about that of our 180,000 physicians, or our 174,000 lawyers. And we surely should not neglect the 1,300,000 truck drivers, or the 2,000,000 sales clerks, or the 900,000 carpenters, even though we also must give proper attention to the qualifications of our 67,000 chemists, 73,000 dentists, 519,000 engineers, and 286,000 teachers. The point is that, among our young men not planning to go to college, very large numbers each year select occupations on the basis of information often fragmentary in terms of both the occupation and its requirements, and their own characteristics and needs.

A large part of this relative neglect of the needs of high school graduates, and of men contemplating entry into occupations not requiring college training, is perhaps due to the heavy concentration of American psychologists in college and university settings. Here the problems that confront them, and place demands on them far greater than they are able to meet, are essentially those of college students. The most interesting problems become those of successful college students; the dropouts tend to enter the occupations below the professional level, thereby vanishing from the view of the college professor of psychology.

I do not mean to give the impression that no work is being done on non-college occupations, for such certainly is not the case. The demands of industry and the needs of the military service have in recent years provided a strong impetus for work with the occupations which are not professional in nature. But it is quite possible that the total amount of attention paid to the selection of medical school students and of life insurance salesmen (who are treated in this report as essentially professional or managerial) is actually greater than that paid to the selection of workers in all skilled and semi-skilled occupations put together. In the field of interest research, with which this volume concerns itself, this is certainly the case.

I contend that this emphasis is not only unfortunate, but seriously mistaken in view of the returns possible in the way of improved utilization of nonprofessional personnel. We commonly think of the professional occupations as those that provide the leaders of the community, both intellectually and socially. We also tend, without much thought, to identify workers in such occupations as printing, electronics, automotive repair, or baking as persons who are a sizable cut below college graduates both in brightness and in level of information. Such impressions do not always fit the facts. The summary by Stewart (1947) of the median scores on the Army General Classification Test (GCT) of men in various occupations requires close scrutiny. These data show many above-average median scores for workers in occupations normally thought of as requiring only minimal intellectual levels. The highest median scores reported by Stewart were obtained by accountants (a median of 129), personnel clerks (128), chemists (127), writers (126), statistical clerks (125), and teachers, lawyers, and auditors (124). Yet draftsmen (120), tabulating machine operators (120), radio repairmen (117), toolmakers (112), printers (111), machinists (110), sales clerks (109), electricians (109), and cabinetmakers (108) all scored substantially above average. The lowest median for any group ordinarily identified as one of the skilled trades was obtained by general painters (99).

One also needs only to call upon his own experience with community endeavors to remind himself that those who take the greatest interest in public school affairs, in local political activities, and in such matters as ur-

The Measurement of Interests

ban development, fluoridation of water, or low-cost housing are not uniformly professional men and women. Persons of strong convictions, of great influence, of wisdom and intelligence, and with great drive and energy, can be found at all occupational levels. A strong democratic tradition requires us to attend to the needs and the possible contributions of persons at all levels.

Our secondary school system can probably not be expected to invest as much money per person in the counseling of high school students as is done at the college level. The resources for such work do not exist, and it seems rather unlikely that either funds or personnel will become available in the near future. We probably cannot expect many highly trained personnel at the high school level. But we do have every reason to ask that high school counseling instruments be as well developed and of as great diversity as those used at the college level. In fact, with male high school graduates annually numbering about 680,000 as contrasted to about 198,000 male college graduates, we should expect a much greater supply of tests and other devices for high school students.

One possible objection even to such an investment of research time and effort as that involved in developing tests for high school students is grounded in the pervasive belief that the great bulk of occupations require about the same minimum levels of ability; that one person will be about as good as another in a given job; that most of the time the major problem is to avoid hiring the misfit who shows up perhaps once in every ten applicants. The best procedure, it would be argued, is to let persons drift about a bit until they settle on something, not too forbidding in character, which uses their skills about as well as could be expected. The current emphasis on security, on uniform treatment of employees, and on wage policies that assure workers of about the same take-home pay regardless of the kind of work they do, seems to be based in part on this view.

This rather cynical attitude overlooks the degree to which very large numbers of American workers take pride in their work, and are remarkably more effective because of their own involvement in the activities at hand. No casual observer of men at work on even fairly routine tasks can fail to see the wide differences among workers in their attitudes toward the work and in their production. Efforts to improve worker placement might be repaid many times if they resulted in an increase in the number of excellent workers. And we are required to deal with the unpleasant consequences of poor placement — the worker whose inattention or lack of skill spoils ma-

7

terials or increases accident rates, the worker who changes jobs periodically, at considerable expense to each succeeding employer, and the worker who becomes a troublemaker as an escape from his job. (Who is to say what recent history would have been had Adolf Hitler been a contented mechanic instead of a frustrated house painter?)

Also neglected by those who see little need to work with the nonprofessional occupations is the degree of difference among them. The way a lawyer spends his time does not appear to the casual observer to be greatly different from the way a psychiatrist spends his time. Yet we recognize that there are substantial differences between these two occupations in the characteristics of the men and in the nature of training required. How much greater, in both regards, is the difference between carpenters and cooks! In many respects the problem of vocational counseling at the levels below the professions is more challenging and more complex because of the great diversity not only in activities within occupations and in characteristics of workers, but also in the stereotypes about these occupations, and the strong positive and negative attitudes held toward various occupations. In a sense, most professions are attractive to college students, although some may be more attractive than others. Below professional levels, one must contend with attitudes that some occupations are unworthy, or are "below *my* level," or are not sufficiently dignified.

All these considerations suggest the need for greater attention to those occupations which are entered for the most part either directly on leaving high school or after some form of apprenticeship or vocational school training. This volume reports one line of endeavor directed toward those persons who are faced with making a choice of occupations near the end of their high school periods. These are the persons who become the nation's artisans, suppliers of services, the sales persons. They are those who make up the membership of many of the large trade unions. They are not, as groups, very much below the professional groups in average intelligence, if we may trust Stewart's (1947) data. They are not routine bench workers or unskilled laborers. They are not underprivileged, or underpaid, or humiliated by what they do. Rather, they represent the skilled workers of the nation.

This report does not attempt to deal with the question raised by Darley and Hagenah (1955) about the possibility of differentiating workers at the unskilled and semiskilled levels. The data here are based on occupational groups well above the unskilled laborer. Even within the Navy structure, on which substantial amounts of data were collected, differentiating among workers below the petty officer level was not attempted. What this report does indicate in the succeeding pages is (1) that skilled trades groups are different from one another, (2) that these differences are substantial enough to be used in classification and in counseling, (3) that an interest inventory used with such groups can be scored in such a way as to reflect these differences reliably, and (4) that such scores have merit when used in a counseling or classification situation.

This report is, in brief, a summary of over ten years' work in measuring the vocational interests of persons employed at the skilled trades level in civilian life and at the technician level in military life. Major attention has been given to estimating the degree to which men in such occupations can be differentiated from each other on the basis of their responses to an interest inventory, and the degree to which these measured interests relate to success in training, success on the job, and persistence in an occupation.

In a sense, this account is a biography of the Minnesota Vocational Interest Inventory.* In a larger sense, however, it is a scrutiny of the taxonomy of an important section of the world of work, since the examination of worker characteristics inevitably suggests characteristics of the occupations which have attracted these workers. The large amount of data collected in order to develop adequate scoring keys for an interest measure also provides information which shows similarities among occupations and permits the definition of job families.

To develop a carefully validated interest inventory is a mammoth task, requiring a great deal of basic work. One must first develop a suitable vocational interest blank, then collect data and run analyses to determine how responses to this blank are to be scored, and then determine whether or not these scores have meaning and if they can be used with profit in counseling. In spite of the difficulties, the development of an interest inventory for use with persons at lower occupational levels seemed highly worth while. Before the beginning of this investigation, of course, American psychologists had learned to use measured interests in the counseling of those who enter fields of work from college student populations. The Strong Vocational Interest Blank, for example, had become by 1946 a widely used instrument for this purpose. Its keys yield scores that have low correlations with ability measures and suggest the degree to which the activity preferences of the individual relate to the activity preferences of members of employed groups.

* A comparable form of this inventory is available for military use under the title Navy Vocational Interest Inventory.

The Vocational Interests of Nonprofessional Men

But the Strong blank has not gained widespread use in the counseling of persons planning to enter less than professional or managerial occupations upon completion of high school or technical school training. For these persons, who make up the vast bulk of the employed adults in the United States, there has been no interest inventory paralleling the Strong. There are, of course, vocational interest measures that may be used with these persons, but these have not been developed in a manner to portray adequately the existence of markedly different interest patterns among the many varieties of workers in nonprofessional occupations.

The vocational interests of persons in occupations below the professional level might be expected to be as sharply differentiated as are the vocational interests of persons in various professions, as long as one does not attend primarily to unskilled laboring groups, or to persons concerned mainly with routine low-level tasks. The fact that a man is an electrician and that he has had less education than a life insurance salesman would not necessarily mean that the former has any less distinctive pattern of interests than the latter. Hence an interest inventory should prove to be very useful in helping a large number of nonprofessional workers identify a job in which they can find maximum satisfaction.

It might be said that the lower educational level associated with occupations below the professions makes it more difficult to devise an instrument that will reflect the differences in interests among men in varying occupations. If we are wise in the selection of item content, however, the only factor operating here would be the ability of the respondent to read. We would assume, that is, that if the respondents can all read and understand the items, the interests of a carpenter would be as sharply differentiated from those of an electrician in responses made to an inventory as the interests of lawyers and physicians have proved to be. And it may very well be that the interests of technical workers in a field such as carpentry or plumbing are considerably more homogeneous, and hence more readily assessed, than those of persons in the professions. The use of interest measures which has become widespread for professional occupations is also possible and desirable at the skilled trades level. For one thing, occupational mobility among workers in nonprofessional groups is certainly no less than among professional groups. It probably is quite a bit greater. This mobility is costly; it might well be reduced by the proper use of appropriate interest measures. There is, in addition, an evident need to take into account the motivations of a person in determining how his abilities can be utilized in the military setting.

During World War II, for example, classification personnel placed considerable emphasis upon the choice of duty or school that a recruit might make. In certain instances the choosing was an integral part of the classification process. Paratroopers, submariners, Marine Corps personnel, and Air Force pilots had to volunteer for these activities. The degree of choice varied, of course, for many different kinds of activities. Often a man who was equally qualified for training in mechanical and electrical activities would be asked whether he had a preference between these two. A person with the qualifications to be trained as either a meteorologist or an electronics technician might well be given a choice.

Letting an individual select an assignment poses difficulties, however, by the very nature of the military process. The new recruit knows very little about the specialties of the military service. For him to make a meaningful choice requires first that he be well informed about the activities and duties involved in the jobs he is considering. Furthermore, he needs to know something more about himself than he often does, whether he, in the long run, will enjoy one type of work more than another. And these kinds of decisions are made difficult because of the anxiety of the newly enlisted man—anxiety about the nature of the assignment he is going to get, about the likelihood of his being able to get back home on occasion, about the nature of the specific station or ship to which he is assigned, and so on. Thus, very frequently when he is asked whether he has a preference for one kind of training or another, his response will be, "Which will keep me on the East Coast?" or "Which will give me the greatest possibilities for advancement?" or "Which is most likely to get me into actual combat at the earliest point?" These considerations are irrelevant to proper assignment; what they do is to increase error in the classification process.

The same objections in somewhat different form arise in connection with civilian occupational choices. The apparent glamour of certain jobs, the nature of training required, the likelihood of higher initial income, the chances for advancement or security, often are considered much more important than the kind of activities performed by persons in a given field.

It would seem that here is an ideal use of a vocational interest inventory: to summarize the preferences of an individual for specific types of job activities, leaving out all the irrelevant considerations. Such a measure of interest does not require the person to know technical or military terms. Job activities can be stated in terms which will be known to the respondent whether or not he has had any civilian or military occupational experience.

The succeeding chapters of this report describe the various stages in the development of a vocational interest inventory and of scoring keys for use with this inventory. The characteristics of these keys are also examined, and various studies on the psychometric characteristics of keys developed by different methods are sumarized. Also reported is the program for collection of responses to the inventory from a wide variety of occupational groups including civilian skilled tradesmen, civilian apprentice groups, students in technical schools, Navy enlisted men at rated levels, Navy recruits, and men in Navy service schools. The total number of completed inventories available for use in the various analyses reported here is approximately 25,000. Of this number somewhat more than 6000 were from civilian workers in various settings and the remainder from Navy enlisted personnel. The largest single group of Navy men was obtained by administering the inventory to 10,000 rated men passing through all Navy receiving stations during the fall of 1951. Civilian workers were obtained primarily through the cooperation of leaders in AFL trade unions in the Minneapolis–St. Paul area. Substantial efforts were made to obtain a good sample of civilian inventory responses. The distribution of men among occupations is still far from ideal in representation of the varieties of occupations at the skilled trades level in civilian life; our Navy sample is rather well drawn and hence much more representative.

✦ 2 ✦

Development of the Minnesota Inventory

THE principle underlying the use of an interest inventory is rarely stated. Yet it is not entirely obvious to all users. The inventory is intended to abstract from a wide variety of occupations the tasks involved, in order to permit an individual to express preferences for tasks rather than occupations. Such a set of preferences then can be studied to determine suitable occupations. Presumably this process reduces the effects of ignorance about the true nature of an occupation, of differences in prestige of occupations, and of such variables as job availability and income associated with various jobs. Some inventories include not merely lists of occupations and of tasks involved in occupational activities, but also items relating to hobbies, types of persons preferred, and personality characteristics, in the expectation that each of these will be related to occupational satisfaction.

The initial step in the usual investigation of vocational interest is the preparation of a set of items and the formulation of these items in an interest inventory. Decisions at this point about item content, item form, or item arrangements are made without benefit of later experience, are made in considerable part on the basis of hunches of the investigator, and yet are critical since they limit the possible outcomes of research with the inventory. Any needed items omitted at the start, for example, can be added later only if the earlier data collection is repeated.

Items of the Minnesota Vocational Interest Inventory (MVII) were written in late 1946 and early 1947. They were so phrased that they could be used to estimate the degree to which either a recently recruited, uninformed enlisted man would like the tasks involved in each of the many

13

The Vocational Interests of Nonprofessional Men

Navy ratings or a youth of high school age would like the work involved in each of a wide variety of occupations below the professional level. The joint purpose was established in order that work with Navy men might be adapted for civilian groups as well and work with civilian groups might be related to that with Navy men. The inventory thus was prepared in two forms with identical item content; the forms differ only with respect to title and cover page.

The items were written with the hope that the effects on responses of intelligence, as well as of special abilities and technical competencies deriving from job experience, would be minimal. Presumably selections among item responses reflect the preferences a man has for given activities in comparison with competing activities. Nevertheless, it is undoubtedly true that intelligence and skill are tapped by these items, if only because some items use technical terms that are presumed to be known to interested persons, but not to all persons. Evidence cited later does suggest, however, that intelligence and ability measures are not highly related to the scoring keys for this inventory.

An obvious source for guidance in a task such as this is the content of other inventories already available. It is immediately apparent to anyone who examines interest inventories, however, that there is great variety in content of items. The Strong and Kuder vocational interest inventories, for example, contain a large proportion of items dealing with actual statements of preferences for different occupations. Many of their other items deal with subordinate aspects of these same occupations. Definitely, these blanks can be called *vocational* interest blanks. Even the Strong blank, however, includes a substantial number of items usually identified with *personality* measurement.

Many of the other inventories in the field are not merely so restricted in content. The items included by Kelley (1944) in his Activity Preference Test, for example, are not vocationally oriented. Some concern the geographic, climatic, and other conditions of the respondent's home at age fifteen and a half, others inquire about sports, or games played at home, others ask whether or not the respondent was responsible for the care of chickens or pigs or a sick person or a shop or a store at the age of fifteen and a half. The range in content of these items parallels that of items included in various biographical inventories developed to serve as measures of the same personal characteristics vocational interest measures have attempted to tap.

Development of the Minnesota Inventory

Still another kind of item is that used by Edwards (1954, 1959) in his Personal Preference Schedule. In this schedule, the respondent indicates that he has, for example, a liking to participate in groups in which the members have warm and friendly feelings toward one another or that he feels guilty whenever he has done something he knows is wrong or that he likes to form new friendships. These items are considerably different in nature from those employed in the Strong Vocational Interest Blank or the MVII and indicate a desire to go far beyond the vocational area in the development of interest and preference schedules. As one examines the Edwards schedule, it is apparent that the vocational-interest content is much less important than the personality-test content. Yet, Edwards reports, "The PPS can add a good deal to the vocational and educational counseling of students."

The variations in content of these item pools raise a number of basic questions about the function of the item pool developed in interest inventories. Minimally, the item pool must provide a wide enough variety of possible responses for the respondent so as to permit a description of him on a number of variables. The nature of the variables on which these descriptions are made need not be limited to obvious dimensions associated with vocational choice, except that if this is not done, appropriate evidence that the instrument has value for vocational guidance must be provided. Insights into factors influencing vocational choice may be achieved by analysis of retrospective data such as that Kelley obtains; yet this sort of inventory may fail to serve the needs of the person trying to select an appropriate occupation. To stress the first point for a moment: interest inventories have proved their practical value, even though the dimensions which they tap are not clearly understood. But efforts aimed toward a better understanding of what interest inventories are doing are very much needed. It is the lack of adequate information on this subject that leads to such variation in the nature of items appearing in these inventories.

Closely allied to the problem of the nature of item content is the nature of the response which the individual must make to each item. Do we measure interests better by asking a person to choose between like, indifferent, and dislike as a response, or should he agree or disagree, or make a like-best, like-least sort of response? Should we require responses to include a certain number of likes and dislikes, or let the individual vary in this as he wishes? In one instance the individual may mark like, indifferent, dislike, or agree, disagree, or something else of this sort, using each type of re-

15

sponse as many times as he wishes. In the forced choice the respondent must pick only one item out of a group as the activity he likes most and, sometimes, one out of the group as the activity he likes least. "Open" responses permit one to compare individuals or groups on the number of likes, indifferents, or dislikes, in addition to indicating what activities persons like most and what activities they like least. In the forced-choice technique the number of "like" responses is the same for each person who follows directions, since he is instructed to pick the same number of "like" responses as every other person. Essentially, this item form eliminates the effects of any personal bias to like or dislike everything and assures comparable response distributions for all individuals.

A still further effect needs to be noted. The distribution of responses to items in L-I-D form may show rather striking differences between groups, some groups being predominantly "likers," others "dislikers." This may perhaps be a characteristic not merely of some occupational group but of groups of individuals having in common some particular personality characteristic. The forced-choice response does not permit the demonstration of this kind of idiosyncrasy. This problem becomes more troublesome when keys describe interests in terms of basic dimensions ("homogeneous keys") rather than in terms of occupational membership. When keys are developed empirically, any "like" or "dislike" biases which do differentiate groups are as useful as any other systematic response differences. In the development of factorially "pure" keys, however, these biases generally need to be eliminated unless they define a dimension related to occupational classification. Thus, the manner in which the inventory is keyed is one of the factors to be considered in deciding whether or not forced-choice responses are desirable.

The Minnesota Vocational Interest Inventory was developed to serve essentially as a device for criterion scoring (that is, providing a number of empirically derived keys based on vocational interests of specific occupational groups), but with possibilities for use in the development of other types of keys as well. Its original form has not been changed. It includes 570 items grouped in threes, making a total of 190 triads. The man who completes the inventory is asked to select in each triad one activity he would like to do most and one activity he would like to do least. In this arrangement item responses are a function of their relation to other items in the triad, so that they are no longer fully independent of each other.

Items used in the inventory were selected from a variety of sources to include types of activities performed by enlisted men in the Navy and skilled tradesmen in civilian life. They were grouped in threes in a fairly haphazard fashion with no a priori scoring plan playing any role in determining item combinations. Examples of triads are the following:

a. Be a grocer.
b. Be a printer.
c. Be a shop foreman.

a. Tune a piano.
b. Cook a meal.
c. Change a tire on an automobile.

a. Varnish a floor.
b. Learn to use a slide rule.
c. Repair a broken connection on an electric iron.

a. Putter around in a garden.
b. Take part in an amateur contest.
c. Cook spaghetti.

The inventory is administered without a time limit and may be given individually or in groups. The directions appear on the face of the inventory and are usually read aloud in a group setting. The directions (for the Navy form) are given on the next page.

Each examinee is instructed to put his name and other identifying information on the answer sheet.

After many years of work with an interest inventory developed in the manner just described, I should be able to make some evaluations of form, item content, and organization which would suggest steps to be taken by others in the development of similar forms. Has the item content proved deficient in any way? Has the form of response given trouble? Would a more carefully designed interrelationship of items in triads have provided a more efficient instrument? Answers to these questions cannot be arrived at by scrutiny of the data in this monograph, but come from accumulation of experiences with the inventory.

Would items have been more effective for our purposes if they had been presented independently and marked as Like-Indifferent-Dislike by the respondent? The work of Zuckerman (1953) indicates that the answer to this question should be yes. Zuckerman, however, studied the effect of using a set of items with L-I-D response categories in contrast to the same set of items presented *in all possible combinations* of triads. He found, as one might expect, that the latter procedure was less efficient in terms of time re-

The aim of this test is to show whether you would like or dislike the work in each of several Navy rates. It is not a test of intelligence or ability. It does indicate the degree to which your interests are like those of rated men in various Navy jobs.

On the following pages, you will find many interests listed. They are arranged in blocks of threes. You must make a choice in each block of the <u>one</u> thing you LIKE to do most and of the <u>one</u> thing you DISLIKE to do most (or like to do least).

You are to indicate your choices on the separate IBM answer sheet. For the item you LIKE to do most, make a mark in the "L" (Like) column. For the item you DISLIKE to do most, make a mark in the "D" (Dislike) column. This leaves one of the three pairs of spaces blank.

For example:

      34. a. Write letters
           b. Fix a leaky faucet
           c. Interview someone for
               a newspaper story

On the answer sheet:

These marks indicate that the item "Write letters" is liked most, and that the item "Interview someone for a newspaper story" is disliked most, or liked least. Item b is then left blank.

Work rapidly. Begin with item 1. When in doubt, make the best guess you can about what you like most and dislike most. Be sure to make one mark in the "L" column and one mark in the "D" column for each block of three items.

DO NOT MAKE ANY MARKS ON THIS BOOKLET.

quired than the former. Perry (1953) completed a more meaningful study, in which he compared one pool of items organized for L-I-D responses with another pool of equal size arranged in triads, and found a slight but not consistent superiority for the triad arrangement.

Experience with the triad arrangement has produced no difficulties. One minor disadvantage is that responses to an individual item lose their meaning, since they are produced not merely by that item, but by the positive and negative attractions of the other two items of the triad. The report of Clemans (1956) on properties of ipsative measures (the effect is the same as to

18

remove the first centroid) indicates that serious limitations are imposed when all scales must add to a constant. This *may* be the case when triads are scored; it is not the case for this inventory, since responses are forced, but scoring is not. That is, the individual who completes the inventory must make precisely 190 "like" responses, and 190 "dislike" responses. His choice of responses in a mechanical domain will not, however, place any direct limitation on the magnitude of his score in another domain except in the small number of instances where a given response is scored on both keys, but in the opposite direction. This effect occurs just as easily with free-choice procedures as it does with forced-choice ones.

The item content of the inventory has proved satisfactory, insofar as this is possible to determine. This content is occupationally oriented much more specifically than is the content of the Strong Vocational Interest Blank. A number of studies have demonstrated the usefulness of the Strong VIB as a measure of certain personality characteristics. Two unpublished studies by Dr. A. L. Benton have indicated rather clearly that the Minnesota Vocational Interest Inventory does not work well when the prediction of neuropsychiatric discharge from the Navy or satisfactory adjustment to Navy life is the criterion.

Some difficulties have arisen because of the vocabulary level. These have concerned the administration of the inventory in early high school years more than scoring. If the inventory were to be rewritten at this time, a vocabulary of somewhat lower level would be used, except for those technical terms associated with occupations in which high schools may already have begun some activity.

The use of vocational interest measures usually assumes that workers in a given occupation have in common certain likes and dislikes, and that these preferences are different from those of workers in other occupations. This assumption has been verified for civilian professional groups time and time again. One of the first tasks of this project was to discover whether or not skilled trades groups and men in Navy ratings could likewise be differentiated. Responses to the inventory were obtained from various groups of Navy men, such as fire controlmen, yeomen, and electronics technicians, and men in nonprofessional civilian occupations, such as electricians, carpenters, machinists, milk wagon drivers, and retail sales clerks. Results obtained from the analysis of these responses indicated clearly that the interest patterns of men in different Navy rates and in different civilian occupations have the same sort of uniqueness characteristic of the interest patterns of workers in various professional groups.

The degree to which an individual's interest patterns match those of a group is determined by use of a scoring key for the interest inventory. This key is developed by singling out those responses which are made *more* frequently by the specific occupational group than by men in general (scoring these responses "plus") and those responses made *less* frequently by the specific occupational group (scoring these responses "minus"). How great the difference in response must be in order for a response to be scored is a difficult matter to determine. The difference must be large enough to reduce to a negligible amount the number of chance differences. Yet the number of responses scored must not be so small as to yield a key which is too unreliable for use. Between these two limits it is possible to develop many different keys possessing rather widely varying characteristics.

Many investigators have questioned the use of criterion scoring for interest inventories, basing their objection mainly on the complete empiricism of the approach. In criterion scoring, a new key, these investigators argue, is required for every new occupation, and there is no provision for accumulation of insights into factors which produce differences in occupational groups. When the nature of an occupation changes, it becomes essential that a new key be developed. Kriedt (1949), for example, demonstrated important changes in the nature of psychology and developed a new Strong psychologist key in 1948 to incorporate these changes. How, except by continual examination, does one determine whether other keys require modifications? Has medicine, for example, changed greatly as a result of new chemical developments?

In reply one can assert that every test or test battery aimed at predicting a criterion must be checked periodically to assure that its functions are still being performed. An interest inventory is no different, and should not be criticized or rejected merely because it aims to do as effective a job as it can. This reasoning, while sound, does not attend to one objection to criterion scoring. We are willing to develop predictor batteries in other domains, and to judge them on their demonstrated effectiveness. But we expect every test to have, in addition to its predictive value, some additional characteristic related to a known or assumed dimension of personality. Tests of ability are not named for the criteria they predict, except in a few instances. They are, in the main, designated as tests of verbal ability or perceptual speed. For interest measures, what are the essential personal character-istics to which we should attend?

This issue has become of sufficient concern in interest measurement to have resulted almost in a choosing up of sides. A large number of counse-lors give vigorous support to the Strong Vocational Interest Blank because, in spite of its scoring problems, it provides definite, specific, trustworthy evidence of the degree to which the interests of an individual match the interests of employed workers in a wide variety of professions. These coun-selors become aware of the relationship among scores for various occupa-tions and learn that certain patterns of scores may be expected. (See Darley and Hagenah, 1955.) They thus add, from their own experience, some or-ganization of the data provided by the Strong to suggest the existence of major dimensions of vocational interest. Another very large group of coun-selors gives priority to the use of such instruments as the Kuder Preference Record because they are easy to score and provide measures of reasonable, sensible, psychometrically satisfying dimensions of vocational interest. These characteristics of an individual obviously reflect important values that he holds which need to be considered in helping him plan his voca-tional career. Their relationship to specific occupations is not so easily determined, however. The job of these counselors then becomes one of learning by experience and examination of the literature the way in which these basic underlying traits are combined to describe the vocational inter-ests of workers in each of many occupations.

It is easy to say that the best tests are factor-pure, or that no test score has any meaning unless it relates to a useful criterion. This monograph in-cludes evidence on the relative merits of the two types of keys, and a sug-gestion that the differences between the two approaches are not necessarily irreconcilable. Evaluation of the evidence requires, however, an assessment of one's own way of thinking about vocational interests, and a review of the purposes which one expects measured vocational interests to serve.

The following sections summarize the work which my coworkers and I have done in trying out various methods for the development of empirical scoring keys. The reader will note that our work is strictly empirical, al-though the ideas tried out arise from theoretical considerations. To the extent that interest inventory responses are unique in their psychometric characteristics, our findings are limited in application. It seems reasonable to assume, however, that similar methods of key development would produce similar results when applied to such related measures as personality inventories and biographical records.

CRITERIA OF A "GOOD" EMPIRICAL KEY

For the purposes of this section, a scoring key will be considered good if it does a good job of separating workers in a given occupation from workers in general. Thus, a key for electricians would perform its function well if the distribution of scores of electricians was markedly different from a distribution of scores of men in another occupation, or of men in a tradesmen-in-general group (the abbreviation TIG's is used for the latter). In the following pages, the index of separation of such distributions which will be used is "percentage of overlap." This index gives the number of persons per hundred in one distribution whose scores can be matched by scores in the other distribution. Perfect separation occurs when the highest score in one distribution is lower than the lowest score in the other; in this instance the percentage of overlap is zero. No separation at all can be made if the two distributions are identical. When this occurs, the percentage of overlap is 100.*

The procedure for scoring interest inventories by the use of criterion and reference groups aims to produce scales with excellent descriptive qualities. The selection of items for scoring is done by observing the percentage of persons in the criterion group who select a certain response, and comparing this value with the percentage of persons in a men-in-general or reference group. When the difference in percentages is sufficiently large, the item is included in the key.

This procedure provides a way of scoring an individual's inventory to determine the interests he has in common with persons in a particular occupation. The score he obtains indicates the number of times his responses differed from those of the reference group in the same way that workers in the occupation tend to differ from the reference group. These scales are thus ordinal scales, and have all the limitations associated with such scales. They also possess a limitation not normally considered: high scores do not necessarily indicate increase in intensity or strength of interest, or even, for certain, consistency of interest. What they do indicate is greater conformity to the group response. We should not be surprised to find that some of the

* This is the index of overlap suggested by Tilton (1937). Tilton's article provides tables which may be entered using the difference in means for the two distributions divided by the average of their standard deviations. For other characteristics of this index, see Tilton's article.

Development of the Minnesota Inventory

most outstanding workers in various specialties have low scores on the key for the occupation in which the bulk of their work has been done.

A second criterion used in the evaluation of a scoring key is its reliability. Test-retest reliability for the MVII was obtained by scoring the interest inventories of ninety-eight men students at Dunwoody Industrial Institute, Minneapolis, who took the inventory twice, with an interval of about one month between administrations. This comparison indicates the degree of stability of inventory scores over a relatively short period of time, and can be used to give an estimate of the amount of variation in an individual's score that might be expected with repeated measurement.

Another estimate of reliability may be obtained by using an index of internal consistency. This statistic may be different from the test-retest reliability, since it is affected by the intercorrelations of item responses in one administration rather than stability of item responses in repeated administrations. Computation of this type of measure is influenced by the use of forced-choice methods, and must be modified to account for the forced positive and negative correlations resulting from the grouping of items in triads.

The most frequently used measure of internal consistency, odd-even reliability, is easily distorted by including parts of triads in both halves scored. The magnitude of the effect will be determined by the way in which the triad is split, and the degree and direction of correlations between the split parts. The degree of influence may be seen when reliabilities are computed using odd and even *items* and odd and even *triads*. Only the latter estimates are appropriate.

Computation of either the Kuder-Richardson (1937) indices or Cronbach's (1951) coefficient alpha also is affected by the arrangement of items in triads. Cronbach's index is

$$x = \frac{n}{n-1}\left(1 - \frac{\Sigma V_i}{V_t}\right)$$

where n = number of items, V_i = item variance, and V_t = test variance. Item variance is usually computed as pq. This is appropriate when one response is scored $+1$, and the other zero. When responses are scored $+1$, 0, and -1, then

$$V_i = p_1 q_1 + p_2 q_2 + 2 p_1 p_2$$

where p_1 = proportion giving the response scored $+1$ and p_2 = proportion giving the response scored -1. In triads where choices are forced, so that

23

one item is responded to as like, and one as dislike, with one item left blank, there are six combinations of responses possible:

1. Like a, Dislike b	4. Like b, Dislike c
2. Like a, Dislike c	5. Like c, Dislike a
3. Like b, Dislike a	6. Like c, Dislike b

Any one of these combination items may be scored zero or one or two scoring weights may be assigned to its components, which means that the pair of responses may collect weights of $+2, +1, 0, -1,$ or -2. The computation of the *triad* variance therefore requires the counting of the number of persons giving each combination of responses, and the use of the formula

$$V_i = \frac{\Sigma X^2}{N} - \left(\frac{\Sigma X}{N}\right)^2$$

Since this is a laborious task, it has been completed only for a small number of scoring keys of the MVII. (This count is easily made on a high-speed computer and has been done in later work.)

A different sort of criterion which may be used to evaluate methods of scoring the interest inventory is the relative success of various keys in the prediction of school success, or the prediction of re-enlistment, or the prediction of military failure as evidenced by records of disciplinary action or less than honorable discharge. These methods of evaluation are obviously pertinent to the application of interest inventory scores, but require the passage of a considerable period of time after administration of the inventory. These criteria are not used in this part of the report. One might expect that keys which do a good job of separating groups would be related to keys that are useful for these other purposes, but only a modest amount of evidence can be presented in this report on such a relationship.

In any development of scoring keys based upon empirical methods, there is always the possibility that the differences between groups in item responses are chance differences which, upon cross-validation, will disappear. Accordingly, for each of the keys developed and reported upon here, a second sample has been used whenever possible to determine the amount of shrinkage to be expected. In most instances this sample is best described as one providing information on the validity-generalization of the key, since it is drawn from a new source. Lest shrinkage be considerable, differences in item responses have been used for scoring only when they were large enough to be well beyond the limits within which chance factors would be expected to operate; this procedure seemed desirable since each key is made up of only a small number of items selected from a total pool of 1140 item responses.

OPTIMAL NUMBER OF ITEMS IN A SCORING KEY

Since no adequate rationale for determining a priori the optimal number of item responses to score in developing an occupational key for the Vocational Interest Inventory was found, we attempted to make this determination empirically. Our work was started with the hope that scoring could be done with less effort than is required with the Strong Vocational Interest Blank, which does a good job of separating out occupational groups at a considerable scoring cost, since each key involves weighting many item responses. Strong assigns weights varying from +4 to −4 to as many as 600 of the 1200 possible responses to his blank. Is this much work required?

The first analysis completed to determine how a scoring key should be developed was done with electricians. A sample of 189 electricians from St. Paul was used. Item responses of this group were compared to those of a reference group including representatives of seven other occupational groups from St. Paul (milk wagon drivers, painters, plasterers, bakers, sheet metal workers, printers, and plumbers). A series of scoring keys was developed on the basis of the difference in responses of the two groups as follows: A 6% key was developed by using all item responses with differences between electricians and tradesmen in general of 6 per cent or more; 580 item responses met this requirement. In like manner, a 7% key, an 8% key, a 9% key, and so on were developed. The series was stopped at a 26% key when only 21 items remained for scoring.

The comparative merits of each one of these keys may be inferred from the data presented in Tables 1 and 2. In Table 1, the test-retest reliability seems the most useful estimate of reliability to use, since stability of scores over time is critical. The odd-even reliabilities and the Cronbach coefficient alpha values are also presented, since internal consistency of keys is also a matter of interest. Odd-even reliabilities are reported for both odd- and even-numbered triads and odd and even items. The odd and even item split was made on each scoring key, rather than on the inventory, so that the first, third, and fifth items scored on the 26% key, for example, would fall in the odd key. This method of splitting did result in rather unusual estimates of reliability, since the system permitted several responses to the same triad to appear in the same half of the scoring key. The odd and even

The Vocational Interests of Nonprofessional Men

Table 1. Comparative Reliabilities of Various Electrician Keys Yielded by Four Different Measures

Key	Coefficient Alpha	Odd-Even Triads[a]	Odd-Even Items[a]	Test-Retest
6%	.95	.92	.91	.84
7%	.94	.92	.90	.83
8%	.94	.92	.91	.81
9%	.94	.92	.91	.80
10%	.93	.90	.89	.81
11%	.93	.92	.86	.80
12%	.92	.92	.87	.80
13%	.91	.92	.83	.79
14%	.90	.91	.82	.78
15%	.89	.90	.77	.78
16%	.88	.88	.77	.78
17%	.87	.86	.77	.77
18%	.86	.85	.73	.79
19%	.84	.81	.77	.79
20%	.83	.81	.76	.80
21%	.81	.82	.66	.80
22%	.81	.80	.67	.81
23%	.81	.80	.65	.81
24%	.76	.74	.58	.78
25%	.73	.72	.67	.77
26%	.72	.71	.72	.78

[a] The Spearman-Brown formula has been applied.

triads were split systematically; the odd-even reliabilities based on these keys have more meaning and are obviously more orderly. Table 2 presents the means and standard deviations on each key for the samples of tradesmen in general and St. Paul electricians, and the percentage of overlap of the electricians' distributions with the TIG distributions.

These data indicate the existence of an optimal point in key development, since greatest separation occurs neither at the end of the scale with the smallest number of items or triads, nor at the end of the scale with the largest number of items or triads. Keys with smaller numbers of scoring weights in general are to be preferred. It seems safe to conclude that, as one starts with a short scale, the addition of more items increases the differentiating power of the key only so long as these items contribute more uniqueness than error; as error increases, the standard deviations of both criterion and men-in-general groups increase enough to offset the additional increase in non-error variance contributed by these items.

With a small number of items, some attention needs to be given to problems of reliability. When the only estimates of reliability that were available

Development of the Minnesota Inventory

Table 2. Means and Standard Deviations of Scores of Tradesmen in General and Electricians on Various Keys

Key	No. of Items	Tradesmen in General (N = 225)		Electricians (N = 189)		Percentage of Overlap
		Mean	S.D.	Mean	S.D.	
6%	580	82.71	61.97	139.03	41.34	58
7%	493	76.48	55.55	128.75	36.88	57
8%	402	73.86	47.94	121.07	31.68	55
9%	345	73.00	43.68	116.23	28.56	55
10%	289	67.55	38.98	106.37	25.35	55
11%	234	61.28	32.93	95.54	21.54	53
12%	201	57.29	29.19	88.61	19.01	52
13%	171	49.89	25.61	78.44	16.66	50
14%	140	42.10	21.58	66.59	13.85	49
15%	116	36.51	18.92	58.60	11.63	47
16%	103	32.32	17.06	52.87	10.48	45
17%	87	28.99	14.68	47.35	9.03	44
18%	72	22.60	12.47	38.61	7.65	43
19%	62	19.39	10.35	33.71	6.42	39
20%	55	16.33	9.17	29.63	5.91	38
21%	44	13.93	7.44	25.29	4.97	36
22%	43	13.41	7.25	24.28	4.84	37
23%	40	12.99	6.41	22.91	4.70	37
24%	30	9.54	5.20	17.21	3.36	37
25%	24	9.04	4.21	15.22	2.70	37
26%	21	8.45	3.83	14.23	2.63	37

were other than test-retest, this problem seemed serious enough to suggest the sacrifice of considerable validity in order to achieve minimum reliability. As Table 1 indicates, however, very little stability of scores over time is lost by a radical reduction in the number of items scored.

Independent evidence to support this generalization about the effects of the number of items in a key has been obtained by us as part of another study using the Strong Vocational Interest Blank. In that study the best key was the one with the smallest number of items scored (24 items). It would seem safe to conclude that unit weighting of a fairly small number of items is a desirable procedure for scoring of any set of vocational inventory responses.

The results of these analyses are so striking that it would seem appropriate immediately to move toward the scoring of a very small number of items for each of the empirical keys. There are risks in doing this, however, since the scoring studies reported represent work with only a small portion of the total variance of an interest inventory. Before we conclude that this procedure would be appropriate in all instances a great deal more work must be done. Already there are evidences, for example, that the patterning of responses which characterize electricians is not like that which characterizes persons in clerical and sales fields. This may be an artifact of the data, since the vast bulk of occupations sampled in work with this inventory have been in mechanical and technical fields. It may reflect, however, more fundamental differences which require better understanding before generalized methods for key development can be established.

EFFECTS OF WEIGHTING

The evidence on the comparative merits of multiple weights and unit weights indicates clearly that superior separation of groups can be attained by use of unit weights. Thus, for our data, the percentage of overlap between electricians and tradesmen in general was 37 with the best unit-weight key, and 53 with a key weighted according to the formula used by Strong. The same figures for printers were 40 and 57, respectively. In scoring the Strong blank, using the best unit-weight key placed men in general 3.71 standard deviations below the mean for psychologists in the original sample and 4.03 standard deviations below the mean for psychologists in the cross-validation sample. When Strong's method of weighting was used, men in general fell 3.23 standard deviations below the mean for psychologists.*

These comparisons do not, of course, indicate finally that differential weighting of item responses would not improve separation of groups. In fact, the entire literature on multiple regression would suggest otherwise. What they do indicate is that a simpler scoring system can separate groups as well as the more involved methods used with the Strong Vocational Interest Blank. In the interests of economy of scoring, it thus seems profitable to use unit weights until such time as the superiority of multiple weights is demonstrated.

The definite superiority of unit-weight scoring in these comparisons directly contradicts the evidence for superiority of multiple weighting systems presented by Strong (1943, pp. 625–33). He reports seven comparisons of

---

* These data were obtained from subsamples of responses of psychologists to the Strong Vocational Interest Blank used by Kriedt in developing the 1948 psychologist key. See Kriedt (1949). Kriedt reports that, for the total sample of 1048 psychologists, the means of professional men in general and of psychologists are 3.25 standard deviations apart, with the standard deviation of the psychologist group used as the unit of measurement (p. 484). When identical computational methods are used, the subsample above gives a value of 3.23, a good indication of its representativeness.

Development of the Minnesota Inventory

unit weights with multiple weights, all of which show substantial superiority for multiple weights. These, however, all involve the use of a constant percentage (15%) cutoff for determining when to score in the unit-weight system. The procedures described in the preceding sections of this current report would require an exploration of various percentage cutoff values in the selection of individual items such that the groups are maximally differentiated. Strong does not report the number of items used in each of his unit-weight keys; it is likely that the number was fairly large.

Much more of Strong's case for preferring the multiple-weight scheme rests on evidence of less than perfect correlations between these keys and those using only unit weights. A large enough number of shifts in letter grades occurs when correlations are below unity to undermine confidence in the shortcut procedure. This shifting, however, needs to be examined only with regard to true scores. Since both types of keys contain error, it is to be expected that correlations will be less than 1.0, and that shifts would occur even if two systems of multiple weights were compared. The critical issue, then, is whether unit weights will ever produce less differentiation than will multiple-weight keys. Strong says yes; in all the studies done as part of this project, no multiple-weight key has approached the best unit-weight key in differentiating power.

These findings would appear to run counter to the known effects of weighting in increasing the correlation of combined scores with a criterion. Presumably we should be able to weight subscores and obtain a better combined score than would be obtained by the addition of the simple subscores. Why should we not observe the same effect when item responses are weighted? Such a question indicates a failure to recognize the limitations of the weighting systems ordinarily used. Strong's procedure, for example, is to give a weight of $+4$ or -4 to those responses which provide the greatest differences between those in a criterion group and those in a reference group. A response made by 70 per cent of a criterion group and by only 30 per cent of a men-in-general group would receive such a weight. This is far from the procedure ordinarily employed in assigning weights in a discriminant analysis, for it attends only to the magnitude of the difference and not to the amount of unique variance contributed by the item. There is no fundamental reason why we should expect this multiple-weighting scheme to have some intrinsic advantage over unit-weight schemes: if there is need to add into the total scale score a more substantial amount of variance from items which have a low correlation with total score, the multiple weights may actually operate to interfere with this effect.

Obviously, some system of differential weighting of item responses should prove superior to the use of unit-weight scores. That such systems have not been developed is probably due to the difficulties of scoring they would entail, and the suggestive evidence that they could not add a great deal to the merits of more simple scoring systems, because they would have to build upon individual item responses possessing quite low reliabilities.* It may be more profitable to develop homogeneous keys and then to determine an appropriately weighted linear combination of scores on these keys for each occupational group, rather than to work with item responses. This has been done in the work of this project; the results are reported in succeeding chapters.

USE OF PERCENTAGE DIFFERENCES

All the criterion key development described in this report uses the percentage of difference in responses of men in contrasting groups as the basic criterion for the inclusion or exclusion of item responses in scoring keys. If 40 per cent of truck drivers respond "Like" to an item, and 22 per cent of tradesmen in general respond "Like," this difference of 18 per cent is the key statistic employed. If the contrasting percentages were 80 and 98, the item response would still carry the same weight and have the same opportunity of appearing in a key.

Many investigators have preferred to employ either correlation indices or significance levels in the selection of items for scoring. The effects appear to be more often injurious than helpful. For one thing, labor is increased. For another, the irrelevant datum of sample size influences the selection of items. For still another, the relative sizes of criterion groups in the sample or the population may affect item selection. Most serious, both correlation coefficients and significance levels give priority to those item responses which have extreme splits in either the criterion or the reference group or both. The most desirable psychometric characteristics result when these items are somewhat discriminated against, as they are when percentage differences are used in item selection.

It should not be inferred that significance levels are not important: serious reductions in group separation may occur in cross-validation samples

---

*The work of Guttman (1947) would suggest that the number of items scored is large enough to reduce to zero any effects of differential weighting.

when one selects a small number of item responses from a pool of, say, 1140 possible responses. Only if the criteria of item inclusion are set at levels well above chance can this effect be avoided. The point being made, however, is that within a pool of items all producing significant difference, it is most useful to select items in such a way as not to penalize those which are responded to in a given way by approximately 50 per cent of a group.

EFFECTS OF INCREASING HETEROGENEITY OF CONTENT OF EMPIRICAL KEYS

The selection of item responses for scoring solely on the basis of the percentage of difference between a reference group and a criterion group will tend, presumably, to give overrepresentation to items reflecting certain aspects of the interests of the criterion group, and underrepresentation to other aspects. Thus, in developing a key for electricians, it might well be that 30 responses indicating a man liked to splice wires, repair circuits, and the like, would be scored, and only one response indicating that a man wanted to study in the area of mathematics, electrical engineering, and physics. Yet both of these responses are characteristic of electricians.

In a sense the use of weights might be considered as an attack on this problem. Most weighting is done, however, on the basis of the magnitude of the difference between men in general and the specific group, rather than on the basis of the amount of the factor already measured by other item responses. To devise an economical procedure for computing such weights directly would be a great contribution — but this project has not done so. In the absence of such a procedure, approximation methods must be employed.

The first method employed in this study to improve the composition of a scoring key was an attempt to avoid including too large a number of items reflecting the central core of interests of an occupational group. An iterative method of item selection was therefore employed. First, the best ten items were selected; these were the items on which the responses of the criterion group differed most from the responses of the reference group. All members of the criterion group were scored for their responses to these items. Next, another ten items were selected for which the difference in responses was still large, but no one of these items correlated with the composite of the first ten items. Another set of ten valid (i.e., differentiating between criterion and reference groups) items which did not correlate with these first twenty was then selected. Finally, ten more valid items unrelated to the first

The Vocational Interests of Nonprofessional Men

thirty were selected. Each key is therefore a fairly heterogeneous key which omits a rather large number of items that differentiate members of the occupational group from tradesmen in general very well.

The first groups on which this type of key was tried were electricians: the sample of 189 St. Paul electricians was used again as an original group, and the sample of 174 Minneapolis electricians was used as a cross-validation group. The tradesmen-in-general sample used as a reference group was composed of skilled tradesmen in fourteen occupations.

The electricians' key which had been developed by simpler means — by taking all item responses with a given percentage difference between the criterion and reference group — was already a very satisfactory measure. The overlapping of scores of electricians and tradesmen in general was only 35 per cent in the original group and 41 per cent in the cross-validation group (see Table 3). Even so, the use of the iterative method for selecting items for scoring reduced overlapping to 30 per cent in the original sample, and to 35 per cent in the cross-validation sample. And this was done without any real drop in the reliability of the key, even though only forty item responses were scored.

Having used an iterative method to ensure that items which contribute new sources of unique variance to the key were included, one might then add back into the key those highly valid items which still had not reappeared in the key. This is the meaning of the phrase "iterative key with best

Table 3. Comparative Differentiating Powers of Scoring Keys for Electricians Developed by the Original Method and by the Iterative Method

Key and Sample	No. of Items	Mean	S.D.	Percentage of Overlap	Test-Retest Reliability
Original key	77				.88
Tradesmen in general ...		22.5	12.9		
Electrician samples					
Original		42.0	7.9	35	
Cross-validation		40.3	8.9	41	
Iterative key	40				.86
Tradesmen in general....		8.2	4.8		
Electrician samples					
Original		16.6	3.3	30	
Cross-validation		16.6	4.1	35	
Iterative key with best items added	62				.84
Tradesmen in general ...		16.2	8.3		
Electrician samples					
Original		30.2	5.4	30	
Cross-validation		29.9	6.1	34	

32

items added" in Table 3. By adding these items to the key, it was hoped that some improvement in the separation of groups would be achieved and that a key of higher reliability would result. As far as the electrician samples are concerned, these expectations did not materialize — no improved separation of any consequence resulted in either the original or the cross-validation sample, and the reliability of the revised key actually dropped a little below that obtained with the original key.

The same comparison of an original key (developed by using all items showing a given minimum difference between criterion and reference groups) and a key developed by iterative methods was made using samples of aviation machinist's mates (AD's) obtained from Navy sources. The results reported are based on a sample of 261 AD's obtained through receiving stations on the east and west coasts and a sample of 292 AD's obtained from the Naval Air Technical Training Command at Memphis. The receiving station group was used for key development, the Memphis group for cross-validation. These two groups should not be considered entirely comparable, since the receiving station AD's were men being transferred from sea to shore duty, while the Memphis AD's were instructors selected on the basis of their AD experience. The Navy men-in-general sample used to determine the amount of overlapping obtained with each key was composed of 200 men drawn randomly from a sample of 1000 Navy rated men selected from the total receiving station sample in such a way as to reflect the distribution of rates in the Navy as a whole. This representative sample of 1000 Navy men in general served as the reference group whose responses to individual items were compared with those of the criterion groups in the development of the original key.

Results of these comparisons are summarized in Table 4. The AD key developed by original methods is not a very good key in terms of its separation of AD's from Navy men in general, since the overlapping of these two groups is relatively high — 65 per cent for the original group and 58 per cent for the cross-validation group. Its reliability is, however, rather good. On the other hand, the key developed by iterative methods is a distinctly better key than that developed by original methods when one looks at the overlapping between groups, but it has a reliability of only .74. These findings are in accord with those obtained with civilian electricians, with the exception that the differences in reliability for the two keys are greater for the Navy sample. (The reader should not generalize from these two groups and assume that Navy groups are consistently harder to separate —

The Vocational Interests of Nonprofessional Men

Table 4. Comparative Differentiating Powers of Scoring Keys for Navy AD's
Developed by the Original Method and by the Iterative Method

Key and Sample	No. of Items	Mean	S.D.	Percentage of Overlap	Test-Retest Reliability
Original key	83				.85
Navy men in general ..		24.3	17.8		
Navy AD samples					
Original		38.6	13.7	65	
Cross-validation		40.2	11.2	58	
Iterative key	42				.74
Navy men in general ...		8.7	6.7		
Navy AD samples					
Original		16.0	4.2	51	
Cross-validation		16.0	4.5	51	

the AD group was selected because it gives relatively poor separation from other Navy groups, and hence tests the value of the various methods developed with the use of the more widely separated groups.)

The evidence thus far presented makes any decision about types of keys to be used rather difficult since improved separation of groups must be weighed against decreased test-retest reliabilities. In hopes of remedying part of this deficiency, still another type of key was tried. The developing of this key requires selection of a fairly sizable pool of items (indicated by percentage differences between criterion and reference groups), and then eliminating those with high indices of internal consistency and only moderate validity. This type of key has been labeled, for want of a better title, the "Gulliksen Key," since the steps taken are similar to those proposed by Gulliksen (1950, pp. 382–85). Specifically, a key is developed by selecting each item for which the response of the criterion group differs from that of the reference group by a given amount or more (generally 12 to 15 percentage points). A large (in the present study, 1000 for Navy, 575 for civilian groups) men-in-general sample is then scored using this key. The top 27 per cent and bottom 27 per cent of this distribution are used to obtain an estimate of the reliability of each item; * the difference in responses of the criterion and reference groups is used as an estimate of the validity of the item. These two values are then plotted against each other much in the manner described by Gulliksen (1950, p. 384), and items are selected much as he recommends. The general effect is to give preference to items which have good validity and do not correlate highly with other items in the pool.

* This procedure is used to yield an estimate of an item's correlation with the total test.

Development of the Minnesota Inventory

It should be noted that this is another approximation method, and is designed to select items having somewhat the same characteristics as the items selected by the iterative method. The Gulliksen method as here used is somewhat easier to employ, is more readily adapted to IBM techniques and hence is a more practical method than the iterative. It should also be noted that the values used here as estimates of reliability and validity of items differ from those outlined in Gulliksen, since in this analysis gross percentage differences are used in estimating those item characteristics.

Table 5. Differentiating Powers of Scoring Keys for Electricians and for Navy AD's Developed by the "Gulliksen" and "Modified Gulliksen" Methods

Key and Sample	No. of Items	Mean	S.D.	Percentage of Overlap	Test-Retest Reliability
		Electricians			
Original key	77				.88
Original criterion sample				35	
Cross-validation criterion sample				41	
Gulliksen key	63				.86
Tradesmen or Navy men in general		13.7	8.5		
Criterion samples					
Original		29.6	6.2	28	
Cross-validation		28.8	6.3	31	
Modified Gulliksen key . .	77				.74
Tradesmen or Navy men in general		9.9	7.8		
Criterion samples					
Original		25.1	6.6	30	
Cross-validation		24.7	6.2	29	
		Navy AD's			
Original key	83				.85
Original criterion sample				65	
Cross-validation criterion sample				58	
Gulliksen key	49				.75
Tradesmen or Navy men in general		12.3	8.0		
Criterion samples					
Original		20.7	6.5	56	
Cross-validation		21.7	6.3	51	
Modified Gulliksen key. . .	64				.63
Tradesmen or Navy men in general		10.5	6.7		
Criterion samples					
Original		18.7	6.1	52	
Cross-validation		19.7	5.9	46	

The Vocational Interests of Nonprofessional Men

A comparison of overlapping and reliability of these new keys with the original keys developed for electricians and the Navy AD group is presented in Table 5. In both instances, the Gulliksen key is distinctly superior to the original key in its separation of the criterion group and the reference group. This superiority is retained in the cross-validation samples as well. In both the electrician and the Navy AD samples this gain is large enough to warrant the use of the new key in spite of the fact that this key has a lower reliability than the original one.

Also presented in Table 5 are data for a "modified Gulliksen" key. This additional modification in Gulliksen procedures is made by adding to the key a small number of items which have zero validity, but high correlation with the items already scored. These items are scored as suppressors. For both types of groups, the modification results in increased differentiating power for the key, but produces considerably reduced test-retest reliability.

(Additional work with suppressor items has indicated that their contribution to increased separation of groups is rather unpredictable. The assumption underlying the use of such items is that there is, in the total variance, a source of stable variance that is unrelated to the criterion. By finding items which have high correlation with this portion of the variance and by subtracting the score on these items, it is possible to remove some of the variance, and hence improve the quality of the key. Apparently in some keys either there is so little variance of this sort or there are so few items that can be used to identify the variance that the use of suppressor items yields no gain in separation.)

Table 6 summarizes the characteristics of the different types of keys developed and reported for electricians and AD's. For electricians, the best key in terms of separation of groups, test-retest reliability, and practicality is probably the Gulliksen key. For the receiving station AD's, the best key in terms of all these characteristics is either the iterative key or the Gulliksen key. Even though the best separation of groups occurs with the inclusion of suppressor items in the Gulliksen key, these items seem to produce too serious a drop in the reliability of the scores to warrant use of the method. (The alternative conclusion, that low reliability has little meaning in a situation where high validity is attained is, of course, a possibility. Had the estimate of reliability been other than a test-retest measure, this would have been an attractive alternative. Even now, it is difficult to interpret the lower reliability; the rejection of these less reliable keys probably reflects the caution of the writer more than it does his good judgment.)

Development of the Minnesota Inventory

Table 6. Characteristics of Various Scoring Methods Applied to
Two Criterion Samples

| Type of Key | No. of Items | Percentage of Overlap | | Test-Retest Reliability |
		Original	Cross-validation	
Electricians				
Original	77	35	41	.88
Iterative	40	30	35	.86
Iterative plus best items.........	62	30	34	.84
Gulliksen	63	28	31	.86
Modified Gulliksen	77	30	29	.74
Receiving Station AD's				
Original	83	65	58	.85
Iterative	42	51	51	.74
Gulliksen	49	56	51	.75
Modified Gulliksen	64	52	46	.63

DISCUSSION

The development of a method of scoring responses to an interest inventory that will permit a maximum separation of workers in an occupation from workers in general involves consideration of many factors. Taking a cue from the application of multiple-regression techniques in previous studies, we would expect that a point would be reached when the addition of more items in a scoring key would not be profitable; that, in general, the greater the heterogeneity of item content, the more effective would be the key; and that the use of weighting methods properly applied would increase the degree of separation of groups. If the criteria of a good key are considered to be its ability to separate groups (as measured by percentage of overlap of distributions) and its test-retest reliability, it is theoretically possible to demonstrate the importance of each of these points. From a practical standpoint, however, one must determine whether or not approximation methods are usable, and, if so, to what extent these various factors need to be considered when employing approximation methods.

Our trial of various methods of developing keys provides support for the following statements:

1. When items are scored using unit weights, an optimum number of items can be found for scoring. For the samples used herein, this number seems to be between 40 and 60; when either more or fewer items are scored, the discriminating power of the key is reduced.

2. When item responses are weighted in the manner used by Strong in

his Vocational Interest Blank, the criterion group is not separated from the reference group as well as when unit scores with the optimum number of items are used. This is not to say that some weighting system could not be devised which would be superior to unit scoring (presumably a set of weights could be assigned using multiple-regression techniques that would yield a score superior to any other score). What this does say is that the method used by Strong is not superior to the method of unit weights.

3. When items are selected so as to increase the heterogeneity of content of a scoring key, the validity of that key is increased, and the test-retest reliability is somewhat decreased. This is true whether items for such a key are selected by an iterative method as described in this report, or by the method of internal item analysis.

4. When an additional set of items is added to a scoring key to serve as suppressors, the resulting key is sometimes better, sometimes no better, as far as validity is concerned. The uncertain effects of the suppressor items may be due to the way in which they are selected — further work is being done on this. Use of suppressor items has, in every instance, resulted in lowered test-retest reliability of the scoring key.

The work described in this chapter has grown out of a need for better understanding of the characteristics of good empirical scoring keys. Since research on interest measurement must place a great deal of reliance on empirical scoring methods, and since the resulting product is judged on the assumption that the best possible scoring has been done, this problem is basic to work of this sort. Early in the work of our project, it was demonstrated that the use of an intuitive scoring key based upon a priori examination of items, and sorting of items into rubrics which would be used for scoring, resulted in a key which was vastly inferior, in use with both original and cross-validation groups, to one developed by comparison of item responses of men in criterion and reference groups.

As additional work was done to determine whether unit or multiple weights should be used, it became obvious that many other questions had to be answered as well. This chapter has summarized the work we have done thus far to settle upon a fairly simple and straightforward method of developing empirical keys for the interest inventory. Our evidence thus far suggests that the most appropriate procedure is one that ensures the scoring of items which sample a variety of different components of an occupational group's interests, and one that is based upon as good estimates of item characteristics as can be computed.

✦ 3 ✦

Characteristics of Occupational Keys

THE preceding chapter has reviewed our search for procedures which would use observed differences in responses of men in various occupations to an interest inventory in such a way as to generate useful interest measures. The keys developed by these procedures permit the scoring of an interest inventory so as to indicate for an individual the degree of similarity of his interests to those of employed workers in many occupations. The development of a variety of such keys permits both a study of relationships among occupations and a study of interrelationships of interests among individuals. Obviously, the greater the variety of groups on whom data are collected the more useful the information about occupational interests becomes.

Not so obvious is the need for a large number and a great variety of occupational groups when scoring keys are developed by these empirical methods. Each occupational group must be compared with a representative cross section of other occupations in order to select those item responses which are characteristic of the group under study. Only when large numbers of persons from many occupations have contributed item responses does it become possible to make reasonable estimates about the characteristics of the general population of employed workers that we want to use for such reference purposes.

In this investigation we have estimated the expected distributions of item responses by pooling data from many occupational groups. The intent has been to obtain a description of the responses of those persons who might be expected to have considered choosing one of the occupations we have studied, so that the resulting scoring key would show how those persons who *did* select the occupation differed from those who *considered* it, but *did not* select it. This purpose suggests that persons of very little schooling and persons with college education should be greatly underrepresented in our cross section, since so few of them would be expected to have given thoughtful consideration to any of our occupations. (For a further discussion of issues related to this point, see Strong, 1943, Chapter 21.) The two cross sections developed for this purpose are referred to hereafter as our tradesmen-in-general (TIG) and Navy men-in-general (NMIG) groups.

PSYCHOMETRIC CHARACTERISTICS OF OCCUPATIONAL KEYS

The use of scores on various keys of the interest inventory with individuals requires that these scores have adequate test-retest reliabilities and low standard errors of measurement. Occupational keys for this inventory have been developed with primary emphasis on validity, to provide the greatest separation between distributions of scores of men in a given rating or occupation and men in general. Even so, it is also important for these keys to have test-retest reliabilities high enough to indicate that some relatively stable personality characteristic is being measured. The relevant data on reliability for each of thirteen Navy keys and seventeen civilian keys are presented in Table 7. Standard errors of measurement have been computed for each key, using the standard deviation of the distribution of scores of men in the criterion group.

Since interest scores are frequently used in combinations, as well as singly, it is helpful to know the correlations between keys. These correlations can be used to reduce the number of keys scored, if there are some keys which are highly related to others. In our work with Navy keys, an analysis of correlations permitted a reduction of nineteen keys to thirteen; the data presented in this chapter are for the reduced number of keys. No reduction in the number of civilian keys has been made. Correlations among keys for a sample of 400 Navy men in general are presented in Tables 8 and 9. Table 10 presents correlations between the two sets of keys. Table 11 presents the means and standard deviations of scores on all keys for this sample.

The correlations among these scoring keys provide useful information about the degree of similarity of employees in various parts of the work force. The correlations among occupations in the building trades are high, for example, reflecting in our data perhaps an even closer association than

Characteristics of Occupational Keys

Table 7. Reliabilities and Standard Errors of Measurement for Thirteen Basic Navy Keys and Seventeen Civilian Keys

Name of Key	No. of Items	Test-Retest Reliability[a]	Standard Error of Measurement[b]
Navy Keys			
AD (aviation machinist's mate)	49	.75	1.51
BM (boatswain's mate)	72	.73	3.74
CS (commissaryman)	62	.81	4.88
CT (communication technician)	60	.81	3.79
DC (damage controlman)	68	.79	3.90
EM (electrician's mate)	67	.87	3.61
ET (electronics technician)	71	.86	3.29
FC (fire controlman)	60	.80	3.94
GM (gunner's mate)	68	.85	3.56
HM (hospitalman)	69	.84	6.60
QM (quartermaster)	65	.74	4.69
RD (radarman)	69	.82	2.97
SK (storekeeper)	64	.88	5.16
Civilian Keys			
Baker	63	.81	3.66
Carpenter	69	.73	2.29
Electrician	63	.86	2.32
IBM operator	93	.83	4.62
Machinist	66	.83	2.89
Mechanic	70	.88	2.98
Milk wagon driver	68	.89	3.12
Painter	63	.84	2.76
Plasterer	66	.71	2.58
Plumber	63	.75	3.05
Pressman	61	.65	2.72
Printer	76	.87	4.25
Retail sales clerk	50	.88	3.74
Sheet metal worker	66	.83	2.31
Shipping and stock clerk	66	.73	4.88
Truck driver	69	.76	3.14
Warehouseman	64	.78	3.38

[a] The data were based on two testings thirty days apart of 98 technical students at Dunwoody Institute in Minneapolis.
[b] Based on the standard deviations of the criterion group distributions.

students of the world of work might suggest. These correlations must be interpreted with some caution, for they are affected by the diversity of interests among the 400 Navy men used. Persons not greatly interested in either plumbing or electrical work will make similar scores on both plumber and electrician keys; the average electrician does not, however, score very high on the plumber key. Data on mean differences will give somewhat different images of the world of work than are provided by these correlation tables.

Table 8. Correlations among Thirteen Navy Keys for a Sample of 400 Navy Men in General

Key	AD	BM	CS	CT	DC	EM	ET	FC	GM	HM	QM	RD	SK
AD ...		.01	-.35	-.72	.27	.31	-.13	.14	.76	-.29	-.55	-.22	-.67
BM ...			.37	-.32	.49	-.39	-.57	-.53	.30	-.08	-.09	-.39	-.06
CS ...				.05	-.00	-.26	-.15	-.28	-.26	.22	.16	-.04	.21
CT ...					-.48	-.16	.33	.05	-.79	.16	.69	.39	.65
DC ...						-.40	-.67	-.50	.42	-.10	-.22	-.47	-.18
EM ...							.65	.82	.33	-.22	-.34	.47	-.50
ET ...								.77	-.31	.11	.15	.63	-.17
FC ...									.11	-.20	-.22	.50	-.25
GM ..										-.37	-.70	-.30	-.61
HM ..											.31	-.20	.06
QM ..												.29	.34
RD ...													-.05
SK ...													

Table 9. Correlations among Seventeen Civilian Keys for a Sample of 400 Navy Men in General

Key	Bak.	Carp.	Elec.	IBM	Mach.	Mech.	MWD	Paint.	Plast.	Plumb.	Press.	Print.	RSC	SMW	SSC	TD	Whm.
Bak. ..		-.25	-.38	.43	-.61	-.62	.69	-.06	-.00	-.63	-.16	.45	.62	-.62	.57	-.09	.41
Carp. ..			-.20	-.20	.03	.19	-.23	.45	.43	.30	-.10	-.23	-.23	.38	-.21	.15	-.10
Elec. ..				-.44	.41	.60	-.51	-.21	-.21	.34	.15	-.55	-.60	.32	-.54	.29	-.50
IBM ...					-.42	-.72	.71	-.31	-.28	-.65	-.07	.73	.82	-.68	.84	-.45	.46
Mach. ..						.65	-.70	-.03	-.05	.49	.26	-.45	-.57	.60	-.52	-.07	-.64
Mech. ..							-.83	-.00	.15	.73	.00	-.82	-.88	.78	-.78	.50	-.44
MWD ..								-.15	-.12	-.67	-.22	.64	.87	-.79	.76	-.26	.55
Paint. ..									.33	.09	.11	-.09	-.11	.18	-.24	-.04	-.15
Plast. ..										.33	-.30	-.34	-.20	.37	-.16	.30	.05
Plumb. ..											-.12	-.73	-.73	.81	-.72	.38	-.36
Press. ..												.23	-.08	-.02	-.15	-.38	-.44
Print. ..													.80	-.72	.72	-.61	.30
RSC ...														-.79	.84	-.45	.50
SMW ..															-.72	.32	-.48
SSC ...																-.33	.59
TD																	.13
Whm. ..																	

Table 10. Correlations among Thirteen Navy Keys and Seventeen Civilian Keys for a Sample of 400 Navy Men in General

Key	AD	BM	CS	CT	DC	EM	ET	FC	GM	HM	QM	RD	SK
Bak.	-.56	.27	.77	.37	-.17	-.34	-.11	-.27	-.46	.16	.32	.03	.53
Carp.	.28	.32	-.14	-.36	.63	-.27	-.45	-.33	.33	-.18	-.15	-.36	-.19
Elec.	.34	-.36	-.28	-.15	-.41	.92	.68	.80	.30	-.21	-.24	.48	-.58
IBM	-.66	-.22	.13	.74	-.29	-.43	.05	-.11	-.73	.08	.46	.11	.87
Mach.	.59	-.34	-.36	-.39	.02	.38	.27	.34	.31	.03	-.33	.00	-.56
Mech.	.85	-.07	-.39	-.72	.16	.58	.09	.41	.79	-.38	-.68	-.03	-.73
MWD	-.77	.12	.47	.58	-.21	-.48	-.11	-.30	-.63	.27	.43	.01	.78
Paint.	.08	.35	.14	-.29	.63	-.28	-.29	-.37	-.10	.07	.07	-.14	-.29
Plast.	.26	.46	.16	-.43	.51	-.24	-.46	-.37	.34	.01	-.14	-.40	-.17
Plumb.	.67	.12	-.35	-.70	.28	.28	-.09	.08	.69	-.16	-.50	-.26	-.67
Press.	-.01	-.31	-.14	.11	-.10	.18	.23	.17	-.13	.13	.19	.25	-.19
Print.	-.69	-.11	.17	.74	-.19	-.50	-.08	-.32	-.74	.18	.61	.13	.70
RSC	-.78	-.04	.35	.70	-.20	-.59	-.11	-.37	-.78	.30	.58	.02	.85
SMW	.77	.08	-.32	-.72	.38	.29	-.14	.08	.69	-.27	-.50	-.21	-.71
SSC	-.70	-.05	.27	.73	-.25	-.51	-.08	-.28	-.71	.19	.53	.04	.87
TD	.38	.33	.03	-.48	.05	.29	-.10	.11	.54	-.30	-.47	-.12	-.33
Whm.	-.40	.22	.15	.27	.02	-.44	-.35	-.33	-.18	.01	.08	-.21	.65

43

The Vocational Interests of Nonprofessional Men

Table 11. Means and Standard Deviations of 400 Navy Men
in General for Various Scoring Keys

Key	Mean	S.D.
Navy Keys		
AD	12.1	8.3
BM	−1.9	7.1
CS	−11.7	9.2
CT	−6.0	9.7
DC	−0.7	9.1
EM	10.5	11.2
ET	1.8	10.1
FC	4.9	8.9
GM	15.6	11.5
HM	−0.1	12.4
QM	−7.4	8.4
RD	−1.8	7.0
SK	−8.9	14.1
Civilian Empirical Keys		
Baker	−8.01	8.24
Carpenter	10.50	6.59
Electrician	15.15	10.54
IBM Operator	−5.71	16.54
Machinist	9.45	8.44
Mechanic	25.28	13.84
Milk wagon driver	−13.19	11.41
Painter	.88	6.66
Plasterer	3.60	5.33
Plumber	13.44	8.03
Pressman	2.80	5.81
Printer	−8.90	12.46
Retail sales clerk	−13.69	11.84
Sheet metal worker	10.22	9.41
Shipping and stock clerk	−11.83	9.44
Truck driver	13.06	7.29
Warehouseman	−4.04	7.06

Another necessary item for the proper use of these interest scores is a measure of the relative degree to which each key performs its presumed function of separating men in a rating or occupation from men in general. The index used to indicate this kind of validity of keys is "percentage of overlap." In our work with Navy samples we have called men in a rating the "original criterion group"; Navy men in general we have called the "reference group" or "Navy men-in-general group." The latter is the sample of 200 men taken from a list of 1000 men drawn to match the distribution of ratings in the total Navy at the time of administration of the inventories. Whenever a cross-validation group was available, either because the sample

44

of men in a rating was large enough to warrant splitting it, or because another sample was available, it was scored on the relevant key. This cross-validation group thus permits a check on the degree to which the empirical key succeeds as a discriminator between groups.

The number of men in each sample, and the source of cross-validation samples, together with the measure of discriminating power (percentage of overlap), are presented in Table 12. The measure of overlapping is the same measure used in the preceding chapter; it gives the number of persons per hundred in one distribution whose scores can be matched by scores in the other distribution. Perfect separation occurs when the highest score in one distribution is lower than the lowest score in the other; in this instance the percentage of overlap is zero. No separation at all can be made if the two distributions have equal means: the percentage of overlap is 100.

It is critical in studying the observed differences in the vocational interests of employed workers to note that the percentage of overlap that we are using to indicate the magnitude of the differences is only a crude index which obscures many interesting and useful relationships. This can be illustrated by examining the scores on a single key made by persons in various occupations — for example, a key for electricians, which has a small number of items. It separates electricians from other workers with a percentage of overlap of 36. Let us look at a few mean scores:

	Mean		Mean
Electricians	31.7	Milk wagon drivers	20.7
Tradesmen in general	22.0	Printers	19.5
Electrician apprentices	28.4	Retail sales clerks	17.7
Machinists	24.3	Navy musicians	17.5
Plumbers	23.1	Navy personnelmen	13.5

These relationships emphasize the degree to which the index of overlapping is affected by the nature of the reference group. Our analyses have employed comparison groups which sometimes include many occupational groups quite similar to those whose keys are being tested and sometimes only a few such groups. It would be improper to conclude, for example, that the commissaryman key is a great deal better than the machinist key on the basis of the observed difference in the percentage of overlap indices.

Each of the keys listed in Table 12 does a very satisfactory job of separating the criterion from the reference group. The poorest job, as indicated by highest percentages of overlap, is done by the GM (gunner's mate) key among the Navy keys and by the shipping and stock clerks among the civil-

Table 12. Validity Data on Thirteen Basic Navy Keys and Seventeen Civilian Keys

	Reference Group			Criterion Groups							
				Original Group				Cross-Validation Group			
Key	No.	Mean	S.D.	No.	Mean	S.D.	Percentage of Overlap	No.	Mean	S.D.	Percentage of Overlap
				Navy Keys							
AD	200	12.3	8.0	261	20.7	6.5	56	292	21.7	6.3	51
BM	186	-2.2	7.3	367	6.8	7.2	53				
CS	200	-12.3	9.4	281	7.4	11.4	34	154	6.6	11.2	36
CT	200	-5.6	9.6	126	6.6	8.7	50				
DC	197	-1.6	8.9	189	11.6	8.5	45	124	12.5	8.5	42
EM	200	10.8	11.5	250	24.4	8.5	50	46	22.6	10.0	58
ET	200	2.0	10.2	217	19.4	8.6	35	46	19.5	8.8	36
FC	200	5.4	8.8	274	16.8	9.2	53	246	18.4	8.8	46
GM	200	14.9	11.4	300	24.6	9.4	64	309[a]	21.7	10.3	76
								(50)	(24.2)	(8.0)	(63)
HM	200	-0.6	12.3	239	25.1	17.2	38	212	25.0	16.5	37
QM	200	-8.3	8.8	195	3.5	8.7	50	42	3.2	9.2	53
RD	197	-1.7	6.9	144	8.0	6.4	47	141	4.3	7.0	67
SK	200	-8.2	14.4	146	13.9	14.9	45				

46

				Civilian Keys							
Baker	225	−11.2	7.1	115	0.5	8.4	45	174	28.8	6.3	31
Carpenter	225	10.6	4.4	313	16.6	4.4	49	86	17.7	11.2	20
Electrician	275	13.7	8.5	189	29.6	6.2	28				
IBM operator	300	−12.9	12.6	107	14.2	14.9	32				
Machinist	225	10.5	8.6	223	22.8	7.0	43				
Mechanic	225	27.7	12.7	162	40.3	88.6	55				
Milk wagon driver...	225	−16.3	9.7	152	−1.5	9.4	43				
Painter	225	2.9	7.1	201	15.4	6.9	37				
Plasterer	225	5.0	5.4	72	14.8	4.8	34				
Plumber	225	14.2	6.8	172	24.0	5.5	43	225[a]	21.9	6.3	56
								(237)	(21.8)	(5.9)	(55)
Pressman	225	2.6	5.3	80	13.6	4.6	28				
Printer	225	−14.0	10.7	305	6.4	11.9	37				
Retail sales clerk....	240	−18.0	9.0	192	3.0	10.8	29				
Sheet metal worker...	225	11.1	7.6	167	21.0	7.0	49	303	20.4	5.6	48
Shipping and stock clerk	225	−16.0	7.4	225	−6.0	8.8	54	79	−10.4	9.4	74
Truck driver	240	12.2	7.4	172	24.3	6.4	38				
Warehouseman	225	−5.0	7.0	84	5.1	7.2	47				

[a] For GM and plumber the data in the first line under Cross-Validation Group are from the first cross-validation group; the data in parentheses in the second line are from the second cross-validation group.

The Vocational Interests of Nonprofessional Men

ian keys. Even for GM's, however, the means of the two groups are two-thirds of a standard deviation apart, and are about as much separated as one might expect them to be, in terms of the diversity of responsibilities of men in these occupations. (Note that the practical magnitude of the difference is the point under discussion here; the statistical significance of the difference is neither considered nor reported, since even these smallest differences are of much greater than borderline significance. Thus, the difference between the 309 GM's and the Navy men in general is almost seven times the standard error of the difference.)

A further indication of the magnitude of the separation may be indicated in terms of biserial correlation. The use of this coefficient requires us to assume that electricians, say, differ from non-electricians in degree, not kind. (This seems a more reasonable position to take than to assume the two groups are truly discrete.) If we assume that the two groups are equal in size and that they differ in means on an electrician's key by one standard deviation, we can then compute the biserial coefficient. For this degree of difference $r_{bis}=.63$. If electricians represent 5 per cent of our sample rather than 50 per cent, the value of r_{bis} becomes .46; if electricians represent 1 per cent of our sample, then the value of r_{bis} becomes .39. Since in most instances it is very difficult to determine the appropriate ratio of electricians, or any other group, to the total employed group from which they derive, we have been reluctant to use the biserial correlation coefficient as an index of group separation.

Even so, had the data of Table 12 been given as biserial correlation coefficients, the largest would have been over .80 (for the samples of 154 CS's, 46 ET's, and 212 HM's) if the ratio of one group to the other were assumed to be one to twenty. The cross-validation samples, it should be noted, are the preferred ones to use in evaluating the effectiveness of these keys, since the original groups would overestimate the degree of separation by capitalizing on chance differences in response between groups. The surprising thing, however, is that the degree of separation is not much different for original and cross-validation groups — hopefully because the methods used in developing keys are designed to reduce the degree to which chance errors enter into scoring.

SIMPLIFIED SCORING OF THE INVENTORY

The explorations of scoring procedures described in Chapter 2 suggest that an even smaller number of items might have been used in scoring than actually were used. Separation of groups was greatest when a very small number of items was used. The procedures for scoring the keys just described are conservative and cautious, in that conventional standards for reliability have been maintained at the expense of some validity. (Perhaps one should say that these procedures are incautious and radical, since validity merits more attention than reliability.) The choice of an average number of items to score was made in part because the exploratory work done was based on only two occupational groups and in part because our findings run counter to those of workers on other devices of this sort. It is still possible, however, to reduce the number of items scored to observe the effects.

One way to reduce the number of items scored is to select the most discriminating n items, without regard to their nature. Such an analysis was made by Albitz in an unpublished paper. Her keys used 15 items each. This number is very small; probably no one would argue for scoring a smaller number than this. She used two keys for study: civilian electricians and Navy yeomen. Table 13 shows three kinds of 15-item keys: "Random," 15 selected at random from the original pool of valid items; "Type I," the 15 most differentiating in terms of percentage difference in responses; "Type III," the Gulliksen key described in earlier sections of this report. Her findings provide dramatic evidence that we do not require a large number of items in order to effect adequate separation of groups; the data of Table 13 suggest that 15 items are about as effective as 63 or 70, both in terms of validity and in terms of test-retest reliability. Her data also indicate the desirability of selecting the most discriminating items from those available when item numbers are reduced.

Is it possible that a reduction in number of items scored can be accomplished in such a way as to ease the labor of scoring an interest inventory? The reduction to 15-item keys does not save much in scoring cost, since these items include some on each side of an IBM answer sheet, and some that are weighted +1 while others are weighted −1. Each key thus requires four scoring stencils, regardless of the number of items. If 30 keys are used, this means 120 operations per answer sheet.

An alternative procedure in reducing item numbers would be to eliminate all items carrying −1 weights. These items tend to carry slightly less differentiating power than the items with +1 weights; their elimination cuts scoring problems in half. Further, if we could be satisfied that scores on some keys can be fairly predicted from scores on other keys, we could per-

Table 13. Means, Standard Deviations, Overlapping, and Reliabilities of Various Experimental Keys

Type of Key	No. of Items	Men in General			Criterion Group				Cross-Validation Group				
		No.	Mean	S.D.	No.	Mean	S.D.	Percentage of Overlap	No.	Mean	S.D.	Percentage of Overlap	Test-Retest Reliability
Electrician Keys													
Original (Type III)	63	240	15.95	8.99	189	29.59	6.23	37	174	28.79	6.34	40	.86
Random	15	240	3.57	3.94	189	6.62	2.19	62	174	6.51	2.19	63	.78
Type III	15	240	1.12	3.28	189	5.68	2.77	45	174	5.21	2.99	51	.82
Type I	15	240	5.70	3.56	189	10.67	2.36	40	174	10.18	2.58	46	.85
Yeoman Keys													
Original (Type III)	70	200	−5.83	15.66	227	18.22	16.16	45	188	18.06	15.65	41	.85
Random	15	200	−1.78	3.77	227	3.47	3.85	49	188	3.70	3.76	47	.77
Type III	15	200	−.51	3.23	227	4.85	3.94	45	188	5.31	4.00	42	.72
Type I	15	200	−2.58	4.34	227	3.91	4.10	44	188	4.36	4.07	41	.79

Characteristics of Occupational Keys

Table 14. Comparative Discriminating Powers of Scoring Keys Using +1 Weights and Original Keys Using Both Plus and Minus Weights

Key	Original Keys		Keys Using +1 Weights Only					
	No. of Items	Percent-age of Overlap	No. of Items	Criterion Group		Reference Group		Percent-age of Overlap
				Mean	S.D.	Mean	S.D.	
Carpenter	69	49	44	24.80	3.76	19.56	3.92	50
Electrician								
1st group ...	63	31	41	31.74	4.53	21.99	6.23	36
2nd group ...	63	28	41	32.07	4.77			36
CS								
1st group ...	62	29	29	15.05	5.95	5.00	3.90	31
2nd group ...	62	31	29	14.63	5.79			32
HM								
1st group ...	69	38	49	28.99	13.57	9.91	8.44	39
2nd group ...	69	37	49	28.96	12.94			37
Machinist	66	43	42	27.16	4.98	19.37	5.89	47
Mechanic	70	55	57	42.50	7.63	32.24	11.00	58
Plumber								
1st group ...	35	56	23	17.91	3.13	14.33	4.55	64
2nd group ...	35	43	23	18.40	3.32			61
Printer	76	37	36	19.19	5.65	9.44	4.62	34
Retail sales clerk	50	29	20	11.11	4.38	3.13	2.83	27
Shipping and stock clerk								
1st group ...	66	54	26	10.72	3.18	7.19	2.77	55
2nd group ...	66	74	26	8.94	3.56			78
IBM operator ..	93	32	49	28.50	7.22	14.28	5.41	26
Truck driver ...	69	38	46	29.37	4.50	21.30	5.06	40
Warehouseman	64	47	32	15.35	4.23	10.56	3.77	55

haps reduce scoring to a point where 20 stencils would give us almost as much information as can be obtained from the use of 120 stencils. Such a system has been tried; the effects of dropping out the −1 weights are shown in Table 14 for a small number of scoring keys. The basis for selecting these particular keys is reported in Chapter 5.

It is clear that for these occupational keys there is very little difference between the original and the +1 weight keys — the saving of half the work of scoring is accomplished with no more change in group separation than we would expect to occur if we had drawn successive random samples from our occupational populations. Do scale reliabilities also hold up as well? We can argue that this is of little importance, since the evidence on cross-validation of the reduced scoring keys is crucial, whereas reliability is not. However, data are available concerning the relative test-retest reliabilities

The Vocational Interests of Nonprofessional Men

Table 15. Test-Retest Reliabilities of Original Scoring Keys
and Keys Using Only +1 Weights (Based on 98 Industrial Institute Students Tested Twice with a
Thirty-Day Interval between Testings)

Key	Keys Using +1 Weights Only	Original Keys
EL (electrician)	.87	.86
ES (electronics service)....	.85	.86
FS (food service).........	.77	.81
HS (hospital service)......	.87	.84
MA (machinist)	.85	.83
ME (mechanic)	.87	.88
OM (IBM operator).......	.77	.83
RSC (retail sales clerk)....	.83	.88
TD (truck driver).........	.73	.76

of nine original and +1 weight keys. These data, derived from a separate study with a sample of ninety-eight industrial institute students, are presented in Table 15. The quite adequate stability of the more economical +1 keys over a moderate time interval is reassuring.

USE OF SCORING KEYS FOR OCCUPATIONAL STUDY

An interest inventory which provides a large number of keys makes it possible for the counselor or other test user to compare an individual's measured interests with those of employed workers in many occupations. The availability of such exhaustive information is sufficiently valuable that many agencies are willing to take the extra time and to incur the extra cost which such a service demands. And there seems to emerge a general consensus that this is the ideal way for interest measurement to proceed.

One major disadvantage of this approach, however, is that it has resulted in a relative neglect of theory development; there has been little effort to conceptualize the structure or dimensions of the vocational interest domain. That work which does emerge in this connection tends to focus on reducing to some order a large number of scoring keys or turns to theory in other domains as a source of hypotheses concerning the measurement of interests.

The value of good empirical keys in the definition of basic dimensions of vocational interests can be illustrated with even a small number of keys. Consider those nine keys presented at the close of the preceding section which sample fairly well some fundamental aspects of vocational interests at the nonprofessional level. Examination of Table 16 reveals a certain

Characteristics of Occupational Keys

Table 16. Mean Scores on Each of Nine Keys of Men in Each of Several Randomly Selected Occupational Groups [a]

Occupational Group	No.	EL	ES	FS	HS	MA	ME	OM	RSC	TD
Machinists	274	24	18	7	9	27	39	14	2	20
Milk wagon drivers....	94	21	15	10	13	15	26	17	8	22
Navy air controlmen...	48	23	18	11	8	17	28	19	5	22
Navy boatswain's mates	366	20	13	12	9	16	29	16	5	23
Navy metalsmiths	210	21	14	10	8	20	35	14	3	22
Navy yeomen	232	14	12	12	9	13	17	26	9	18
Printers	143	20	15	8	12	18	24	16	4	16
Radio and TV apprentices	56	29	24	10	10	17	31	15	4	23
Retail sales clerks.....	128	18	14	10	13	14	23	21	10	20

[a] For ease of reading, all mean values have been rounded to the nearest whole number.

amount of orderliness and organization. From these rounded mean scores of several diverse occupational groups on each of the +1 unit-weight keys, a hierarchy of occupations can be established. This is true even for the food service key which taps a dimension not well represented in our sample of occupations. Furthermore, the patterning of scores reveals the manner in which groups differ from each other and suggests the existence of job families. A vast amount of data of this sort is available from many years of data collection and analysis with the MVII as well as with other interest inventories. It would be desirable to examine such data for theoretically significant regularities.

While the examination of mean scores is a useful exercise, it becomes bewildering when many occupational groups are involved. A more precise understanding of relationships readily develops when statistical techniques are employed to aid in the combination of scores and in the classification of occupations into groups. Such an analysis is presented in the latter part of the next chapter.

✦ 4 ✦

Characteristics of Homogeneous Keys

THE world of work may be described aptly in either of two ways. One is by description of the tasks of workers; these are grouped into clusters of activities called occupations, clusters presumably reflecting the influence of years of experimentation with various ways of dividing workers' duties. The second procedure is to look at the characteristics of workers and to note the different dimensions of abilities, aptitudes, interests, values, and other characteristics which emerge, as these are related to choice of and success in various types of work.

These two modes of attack are somewhat like the two methods of developing scoring keys which are described in this report. The preceding chapter accepts the world of work as it exists and searches for differences among workers in various occupations. This chapter starts afresh, and looks at the way in which workers' preferences tend to pattern. The former procedure develops empirical or occupational keys. The latter develops homogeneous keys.

Homogeneous scales allow, for persons with a clinical or counseling orientation, interpretation of a more complex order than do the heterogeneous collections of items resulting from the empirical approach to test construction. Homogeneous scales are more nearly pure measures of independent traits and by resembling other measures of the characteristics of individuals appear to be more meaningful psychologically than are the collections of items that are scored in empirical keys.

AUTHOR'S NOTE: This chapter draws substantially on the research of Dr. Helen H. Gee of the Association of American Medical Colleges and Dr. Warren T. Norman of the University of Michigan.

Characteristics of Homogeneous Keys

Typically, the development of homogeneous scales starts out by establishing a priori several pools of items that appear to "go together." Statistical techniques are then applied in order to identify those subsets of items which satisfy criteria of statistical homogeneity, and the resulting item collections are labeled in accordance with their apparent content. The Kuder Preference Record is a widely used representative of homogeneous keying.

In the development of empirical scales, on the contrary, item content is considered only during the process of establishing a total item pool, and then it is considered for purposes of obtaining as wide as possible a representation of the kinds of behavior it is desired to investigate. Items are formed into keys on the basis of the degree to which they differentiate between groups, or, in essence, the degree to which they correlate with a criterion. Until recently, this was the major requirement for the inclusion of an item in a scale, the technique being most ably represented by the Strong Vocational Interest Inventory (and among personality inventories by the Minnesota Multiphasic Personality Inventory). As indicated in Chapter 2, the present study has introduced another criterion designed deliberately to assure maximum heterogeneity among items selected by requiring for inclusion in a key, not only high validity in relation to an external criterion, but minimum or negative relationship with total score (thus minimizing item intercorrelations). Scales so formed are identified by naming them for the criterion they have been developed to predict.

Interpretation of a heterogeneous, empirically developed interest scale involves consideration of a person's attitudes, preferences, and dislikes as they compare with those of people who engage in various specific occupations. It is assumed that an individual whose personal characteristics are like those of persons engaged in a given occupation will find satisfaction in that occupation or at least will persist in it. Interpretation of a score thus makes direct use of occupational terms. On the other hand scores on a homogeneous key are interpreted with an orientation toward a *person* rather than an *occupation*. They presumably describe the relative strength, in an individual, of preferences for a number of activities which supposedly cover the major dimensions of vocational interests.

DESCRIBING THE BASIC DIMENSIONS OF INTERESTS

Is it more meaningful to say (1) that an individual has high preferences for clerical activities or (2) that he has interests that are like those of persons who are successful in clerical jobs? What is the meaning and significance of the former statement when an individual does not have interests like those of persons engaged in clerical occupations? DuBois, Loevinger, and Gleser (1952) found the correlation between an occupational key developed on clerical workers and a homogeneous key to be only .52. For the same comparison of the two types of mechanical keys the correlation was .13. For radio operators the correlation was .44. It does not follow, therefore, that a description of the world of work by the use of occupational keys will necessarily yield the same results as the description of characteristics of individuals.

Another line of evidence is available to suggest the same thing. A study conducted at the Institute for Personality Assessment and Research at the University of California involved a three-day living-in assessment of one hundred Air Force officers. These officers had been administered the Strong Vocational Interest Blank and were being observed and rated during the three-day period. One of the records obtained from this assessment was a description of each man in terms of a series of Q sorts. A high correlation was observed between scores from the psychologist key of the Strong Vocational Interest Blank and ratings on the following items: has high degree of intellectual ability; is verbally fluent, conversationally facile; highly cathects intellectual activity, values cognitive pursuits; tends to become ego-involved, makes personally relevant many different contexts; is concerned with philosophical problems, e.g., religion, values, the meaning of life, etc.; communicates ideas clearly and effectively. A set of negative correlations with the psychologist key (at the .01 level of significance) was observed for the following items: has a narrow range of interests; is rigid, inflexible in thought and in action; is stereotyped and unoriginal in his approach to problems; conforming, tends to do the things that are prescribed; tends not to become involved in things, passively resistant.

It is clear that these descriptions of a psychologist are substantially different from a description of psychological activities and also substantially different from the description of a psychologist that would be obtained using those items which differentiate a psychologist from workers in other domains. We should not expect that a person who is well described by the statements in the positive list and very poorly described by the statements in the negative list would necessarily be found employed as a psychologist. What we should note, however, is that any items of this sort which turned out to differentiate between persons employed as psychologists and persons not so employed can be used in any empirical scoring key. The procedures for developing such keys capitalize on any source of variance which permits the separation of psychologists or any other occupational group from employed persons in general.

The fact that high correlations between homogeneous and occupational keys are not obtained serves to emphasize the fact that the interpretative significance of scores on occupational keys is severely limited. The interpretative significance of homogeneous scores is also limited, however. The Kuder Preference Record permits illustration of this point.

The Kuder Preference Record provides scores on a number of relatively independent homogeneous dimensions of interest. If one knows the scores for an individual on the several scales, how much can be said about him beyond the fact that he has greater preference for certain kinds of activities than do those in the normative group with which he is compared? An illustration of the probable interpretation can be given from data collected by Triggs in 1943. With a sample of 166 male college students, she found the relationships among keys shown in the accompanying tabulation. Kuder has provided long lists of occupations presumed to be indicated by high scores on various scales. Many of the occupations listed may be there because their duties *appear* to be consistent with the activities of the scale or scales under which they are listed. It is this *apparent* relationship which must be scrutinized with care.

Strong Key	*Kuder Scale*	*r*
Mathematician	Computational	−.14
Accountant	Computational	.49
Engineer	Mechanical	.72
Chemist	Scientific	.73
Sales manager	Persuasive	.72
Artist	Artistic	.56
Author-journalist	Literary	.28
Musician	Musical	.51
YMCA secretary	Social service	.35
Office manager	Clerical	.38
Banker	Clerical	.62

Kuder has, of course, recognized the need for a more satisfactory, empirical basis for interpretation of scores. He has provided average profiles of scores of persons actually engaged in various occupations and more recently has begun to develop linear discriminant function weights to provide a statistically sound basis for the identification of interests of specific occupational groups. For homogeneous scales to achieve the interpretative significance that is built into heterogeneous scales is both a lengthy and a statistically difficult task. If discriminant function weights are eventually provided for as many occupations as appear on a Strong profile, the test user, to obtain an equal amount of information from the Kuder, would be required to compute 9×42 or 378 multiplications and 42 summations. It is naive to suppose that this would become common practice.

Lacking discriminant weights, we can compare an individual profile of homogeneous scale scores with average profiles of occupational groups only by recourse to subjective judgment or to some index of profile similarity, which again raises extensive computational (to say nothing of theoretical) problems. While the procedures involved in achieving interpretative significance may be statistically more rigorous and psychometrically more orderly for homogeneous than for empirical keying, there is some doubt that the additional labor is warranted. It would not be if validity on cross-validation did not differ for the two techniques.

Homogeneous scales are very attractive because they involve such a small amount of scoring and provide a number of independent scores small enough for the human mind to grasp. The Minnesota Multiphasic Personality Inventory, for example, has achieved widespread use and has had developed for it a variety of profile analysis procedures primarily because the number of variables is small. It is true that the Strong Vocational Interest Blank is also widely used but it becomes much more difficult to interpret in profile form unless one is willing to deal with a much smaller number of underlying dimensions than are reflected in the scoring keys. It is worthy of note that the excellent monograph of Darley and Hagenah (1955) on the use of the Strong Vocational Interest Blank does just this. It engages in pattern analysis techniques which use clusters of scores to identify a single dimension rather than deal with each of the empirical scoring keys provided.

It certainly ought to be the case that the world of work could be described in a smaller number of dimensions than is done by the Strong Vocational Interest Blank. It is probable that the number of dimensions used in the Kuder Preference Record is close to the *number* required. The fact that no blank now exists which describes effectively the interests of an individual in terms of pure factor scores is, however, not at all surprising. The early work of Strong suggested that such a small number of keys fails to provide the sort of separations among groups that is obtained when empirical keys of the ordinary sort are used. It ought to be possible at the present time, however, to work with a small number of factor scores.

Characteristics of Homogeneous Keys

A factor analysis of forty-nine interest variables by Torr in 1953 found eight definable factors. These were essentially as follows: (1) Interest in mechanics. (2) Interest in people. (3) Interest in aesthetics. (4) Interest in nature. (5) Response set. (6) Interest in science. (7) Interest in business. (8) Response set.

A similar factor analytic study was completed by Lecznar, Fruchter, and Zachert in 1951 with the Airman Biographical Inventory. This inventory yields nine factors as follows: (1) Mechanical experience. (2) Numerical facility. (3) Biographical inventory — things vs. ideas. (4) Technical information. (5) Perceptual. (6) Verbal. (7) Biographical inventory — practical vs. theoretical. (8) Educational background. (9) Visualization. One must note that this latter analysis deals not only with vocational interests but with certain noncognitive aspects of an individual.

THE CONSTRUCTION OF HOMOGENEOUS KEYS

It would be useful to have available an inventory and a set of scoring procedures which could accomplish both classes of objectives: those which are achieved using empirical or criterion keys and those which are achieved using homogeneous or factorially simple keys. The intent behind the development of homogeneous keys described in the remaining portion of this chapter was to find measures which would represent meaningful dimensions of vocational interest within an individual and yet permit a counselor to say that a person is like employed workers in a given occupation.

The prototype scales in the procedures about to be described were those developed by DuBois, Loevinger, and Gleser (1952). The procedures employed were patterned after theirs with certain exceptions. The steps in the development of scales are outlined in detail, since the merit of the resulting groups of items is derived from the procedures used in locating them.

Homogeneous scales, as has already been noted, are developed by searching for patterns of item responses that seem to belong together. Two items which evoke similar responses are presumably related to the same facet of an individual; items evoking different responses obviously do not describe the same characteristic. The search for item responses that constitute such patterns employs indices of correlation. When item intercorrelations are high, the items are placed in the same scale; when they are low, they cannot be placed in the same scale. In our project, item covariances could be used instead of item intercorrelations with a substantial reduction in the amount of computation required.

The Vocational Interests of Nonprofessional Men

The 1140 item responses in the MVII provide $(1140 \times 1139) \div 2$, or 649,230, item covariances, since there are that many pairs of item responses. Even with large digital computers at one's disposal, such a considerable number of indices become difficult to work with. In reducing the task to workable dimensions, several possibilities present themselves. Separate sets of scales can be constructed from various sections of the test and later combined, for instance, or a basic set can be constructed from one section of the test and other items added on the basis of their relationships to the original set.

For making judgments about the comparative utility of homogeneous and heterogeneous scales, however, use of the entire test is not necessary. If selection of items for both kinds of scales is limited to a particular set of items, the necessary data for comparison of scales should be obtainable and should be generalizable to the use of all items. Accordingly, in order that a rigorous method could be applied to the development of the homogeneous scales, we decided in the first stage of our comparison to use only "like" responses from the first half of the test. This reduced the total number of item responses under consideration to 288 (instead of 1140) and reduced the number of item covariances to the still large but potentially manageable size of 41,328.

The procedure followed in development of the homogeneous scales differed from that described by DuBois, Loevinger, and Gleser in that our items were not initially classified on the basis of judged content. In our work, no assumptions were made concerning the probable underlying dimensions generating obtained interrelationships among activity preferences; unexpected item relationships, then, could influence scale development.

The entire matrix of covariances based on the interrelationships of the 288 "like" responses (to each item in the first 96 triads) of 400 Navy men was utilized. (These men constituted a random sample from a group of 1000 Navy men drawn in such a way as to represent all men in the Navy in 1951–52.) In order to make feasible the handling of this vast array of covariances, a card was prepared for each of the 288 items. The entire array of covariances for each item was scanned and on each card were jotted the highest covariances with their corresponding item numbers. All positive covariances above .050 were recorded for each item.* (Maximum covari-

*The formula for computation of item covariance is $C_{ij} = p_{ij} - p_i p_j$ where p_{ij} = proportion endorsing both items, p_i = proportion endorsing item i, and p_j = proportion endorsing item j.

ance can be obtained for an item endorsed by 50 per cent of respondents and is equal to .25.) Many items were found to have no covariance higher than .025, but a minimum of ten of the highest covariances for each item was nonetheless sought. In general each item was first studied to determine if it appeared to have any relatively high covariances with other items and then an arbitrary minimum value for the covariances to be recorded for that item was set. All covariances above the arbitrary minimum were recorded. The item's highest covariance with any other item was recorded in the upper right hand corner of the card, its variance in the lower right hand corner. This procedure proved to facilitate the selection of three-item nuclei immeasurably.

The general procedure for construction of homogeneous scales is as follows: The triplet of items with the highest intercorrelations from among all items in the matrix form the nucleus of a scale. These three items plus those added to it as the process continues form a scale in which there is no item which lowers the saturation of the scale. One new item is selected which will maximize the saturation of the resulting four-item scale; any of the four items which would lower the saturation of the scale is discarded. This procedure continues until all items are included in the scale or discarded.

Further adjustments were made in our work by constructing covariance matrices of items for pairs of scales that were highly correlated. The sums of covariances of items in one scale with items of the other were computed and divided by the item variance. This ratio gave an estimate of the relative contribution of an item to the intertest correlation, and use of the covariance matrix permitted rapid re-computation of interscale correlations following addition and subtraction of items to scales. This procedure was found to be highly satisfactory and seemed preferable to correcting point biserial correlations between items and their own keys and to the laborious testing of inequalities to estimate the effects of adding and subtracting individual items as is suggested by DuBois, Loevinger, and Gleser. By working directly with item covariance matrices it was possible to handle several items at a time and to determine immediately the exact effects of changes in the scales on scale intercorrelations and saturations.

CORRELATIONS BETWEEN HOMOGENEOUS AND OCCUPATIONAL KEYS

The homogeneous keys and the empirical scoring keys developed according to the procedures outlined in the preceding chapter were used in scoring the completed interest inventories of our sample of 400 Navy men in general. Since all these inventories were scored on all keys, it was possible to compute interscale correlations within the set of homogeneous keys, within the set of occupational keys, and between sets. Probably of greatest interest are the correlations between scoring keys of the two disparate types. These correlations are presented in Table 17. Also presented in this table are multiple correlations of the full set of nine homogeneous keys with each occupational key and the internal consistency of each key as determined by the Kuder-Richardson formula No. 20.

One might assume that since homogeneous and empirical methods of scale construction employ techniques of item selection that are quite dissimilar in purpose, intercorrelations between homogeneous and "heterogeneous" scales would be low or, at best, moderate. But Table 17 plainly indicates that this is not so. For each homogeneous scale, except the last two derived, H_{9a} and H_0, there is at least one empirical scale with which there is a high correlation. The intercorrelation matrix provides a wealth of opportunity for speculation.

The magnitude of the correlations indicates that very nearly all the nonerror variance in six of the ten occupational scales is accounted for by an individual homogeneous scale. It is important, however, to take into account the fact that the two sets of scales draw their items from the same item pool. Error components of items common to two scales are treated as valid variance and are confounded with the valid relationships between the scales, inflating to an unknown extent the correlation between the scales. While these components cannot be isolated and measured, it is possible to obtain an estimate of the extent to which the observed relationship between the scales is a function of overlapping item selection. Guilford (1936, p. 364) cites a formula for the determination of correlation of common elements which may be applied to these data. The formula expresses the ratio of the number of common items in the two scales to the geometric mean of the total number of items. Table 18 shows the result of these calculations. While these coefficients represent what may be termed a somewhat "oblique" approach both to the concept of correlation per se and to the interpretation of correlation as a function of "elements," they do provide a basis for insight into the relationships between the scales. Some of the coefficients are substantial, but none approaches the level of the product-moment intercorrelations between the scales. Certainly it cannot be said that the observed relationships between the scales can be accounted for on the basis of overlapping in item content alone.

Table 17. Intercorrelations of Homogeneous and Empirical Keys Based on Scores of 400 Navy Men in General and Multiple Correlations of Combined Homogeneous Scores with Empirical Key Scores

Homogeneous Key	No. of Items	KR 20	Empirical Key									
			ADL_1	CSL_1	CTL_1	DCL_1	EML_1	ETL_1	FCL_1	GML_1	HML_1	SKL_1
Multiple R [a]			.80	.91	.85	.86	.95	.86	.99	.92	.88	.93
No. of items			23	28	27	23	44	39	35	38	24	27
KR 20			.76	.76	.80	.74	.87	.80	.78	.87	.83	.90
H_{1a}	26	.88	.77 [b]	.14	.19	.17	.39	-.13	.14	.89	-.45	-.74
H_{2a}	18	.82	-.33	.04	.57	-.09	-.22	.13	-.13	-.47	.86	.05
H_{3a}	23	.90	-.46	-.20	-.02	.00	-.45	-.15	-.23	-.55	.08	.90
H_{4a}	12	.77	.10	.89	-.07	-.53	.90	.67	.79	.41	-.40	-.47
H_5	13	.76	-.22	.08	-.22	.06	-.22	-.05	-.17	-.28	.22	.02
H_6	17	.67	.19	.28	.66	.84	-.72	-.75	-.72	.01	-.04	.11
H_{7a}	16	.77	-.60	.10	.33	-.17	-.25	.23	-.03	-.74	.33	.42
H_{8a}	12	.53	-.30	-.39	-.13	-.04	-.25	-.08	-.19	-.35	.09	.50
H_0	10	.55	.38	.10	-.13	.12	.30	.17	.27	.30	-.14	-.53

[a] Based on the combination of all homogeneous scales.
[b] The largest value of r in each column is italicized.

63

The Vocational Interests of Nonprofessional Men

Table 18. Correlations between Selected Homogeneous and Empirical
Scales of Common Item Elements

Scale Comparison	r^a	Observed r	Scale Comparison	r	Observed r
ADL₁ and H₁ₐ	.24	.77	FCL₁ and H₄ₐ	.39	.79
GML₁ and H₁ₐ	.32	.89	CSL₁ and H₅	.52	.89
HML₁ and H₂	.53	.86	DCL₁ and H₆	.40	.84
SKL₁ and H₃ₐ	.44	.90	CTL₁ and H₇ₐ	.14	.66
EML₁ and H₄ₐ	.44	.90			

a The formula used is

$$r = \frac{n_c}{\sqrt{n_a + n_c} \ \sqrt{n_b + n_c}}$$

where n_a = the number of nonoverlapping items in one scale, n_b = the number of nonoverlapping items in the second scale, and n_c = the number of items the two scales have in common.

If we examine the available correlation information, two conclusions appear to be warranted: First, the magnitude of the multiple correlations of combined homogeneous scores with individual empirical key scores indicates that the homogeneous scales do account for a substantial part of the variation in interest dimensions, and so are potentially useful tools. Second, scales H_1 to H_6 of the homogeneous scales and CS, DC, EM, GM, HM, and SK of the empirical scales are correlated to such an extent as to warrant assuming that they are tapping the same set of interest dimensions.

The set of homogeneous keys producing the correlations in Tables 17 and 18 is a preliminary set using only those items drawn from the first half of the interest inventory. These were developed by Gee (1955). A second set of homogeneous keys was then developed by Norman (1957). His revised keys were prepared by computing the point biserial correlations between items in both halves of the interest inventory and the original preliminary homogeneous keys. The augmented pool of items permitted some increase in length and some improvement in the characteristics of the homogeneous keys, and also provided for a second comparison of the characteristics of homogeneous keys and those of the empirical keys developed from the entire pool of items in the inventory.

The characteristics of the preliminary and the final homogeneous keys, and the intercorrelations among the final keys, are presented in Tables 19 and 20. The data in the latter table reflect the comparative success in developing homogeneous keys which are relatively independent of each other

Characteristics of Homogeneous Keys

Table 19. Characteristics of Preliminary and Final
Homogeneous Keys

Key	No. of Items	400 Navy Men in General	
		Mean	S.D.
Preliminary (Gee) Keys			
H_{1a}	26	14.32	6.40
H_{2a}	18	4.48	3.80
H_{3a}	23	4.24	4.77
H_{4a}	12	5.45	3.16
H_5	13	2.86	2.62
H_6	17	5.53	3.04
H_{7a}	16	3.21	2.93
H_{9a}	12	2.53	1.91
H_0	10	4.63	2.08
Final (Norman) Keys			
H_{1b}	22	12.31	6.34
H_{2b}	22	5.08	5.08
H_{3b}	21	4.62	5.16
H_{4b}	18	8.53	4.74
H_{5b}	20	5.02	3.84
H_{6b}	19	7.29	3.88
H_{7b}	19	4.70	3.94
H_{9b}	18	4.72	3.08
H_{0b}	16	8.55	3.13

Table 20. Correlations among Nine Final Homogeneous Keys for a
Sample of 400 Navy Men in General

Key	H_{1b}	H_{2b}	H_{3b}	H_{4b}	H_{5b}	H_{6b}	H_{7b}	H_{9b}	H_{0b}
H_{1b}		−.42	−.69	.58	−.27	.07	−.72	−.52	.63
H_{2b}	−.42		−.07	−.30	.21	−.22	.38	.03	−.29
H_{3b}	−.69	−.07		−.38	−.12	−.03	.43	.54	−.48
H_{4b}	.58	−.30	−.38		−.18	−.53	−.35	−.22	.34
H_{5b}	−.27	.21	−.12	−.18		.01	.21	.00	−.35
H_{6b}	.07	−.22	−.03	−.53	.01		−.20	−.11	.16
H_{7b}	−.72	.38	.43	−.35	.21	−.20		.34	−.57
H_{9b}	−.52	.03	.54	−.22	.00	−.11	.34		−.37
H_{0b}	.63	−.29	−.48	.34	−.35	.16	−.57	−.37	

(compare this table, for example, with Tables 8, 9, and 10 in the preceding chapter).

Relationships between the revised homogeneous keys and the Navy and civilian empirical keys are presented in the correlation matrices of Tables 21 and 22. The phenomenon already noted of the high relationships between certain paired homogeneous and empirical keys is again observable in these tables, where the keys used are based on the item content of the entire inventory.

Table 21. Correlations among Nine Final Homogeneous Keys and Nineteen Civilian Keys for a Sample of 400 Navy Men in General

Key	H_{1b}	H_{2b}	H_{3b}	H_{4b}	H_{5b}	H_{6b}	H_{7b}	H_{9b}	H_{0b}
Baker	−.58	.14	.38	−.30	.66[a]	−.08	.39	.39	−.52
Carpenter	.20	−.22	−.16	−.23	−.09	.62	−.30	−.18	.28
Electrician ...	.56	−.13	−.47	.89	−.11	−.53	−.32	−.30	.32
IBM operator .	−.79	.11	.85	−.42	.03	−.08	.61	.52	−.54
Machinist	.52	.05	−.43	.26	−.25	−.03	−.32	−.38	.26
Mechanic	.90	−.40	−.63	.60	−.30	.03	−.71	−.48	.62
Milk wagon driver	−.83	.25	.62	−.46	.35	−.07	.57	.50	−.55
Painter	.07	.03	−.31	−.26	.20	.53	−.04	−.31	.06
Plasterer	.18	−.07	−.26	−.26	.14	.47	−.26	−.16	.25
Plumber	.69	−.16	−.61	.24	−.24	.19	−.59	−.49	.71
Pressman	.04	.15	−.10	.12	−.05	−.12	.15	−.08	−.15
Printer	−.78	.20	.67	−.49	.10	−.05	.71	.50	−.58
Retail sales clerk	−.91	.29	.75	−.58	.25	−.04	.70	.53	−.65
Sheet metal worker	.76	−.29	−.62	.25	−.21	.27	−.63	−.45	.60
Shipping and stock clerk ...	−.84	.18	.79	−.49	.15	−.07	.61	.58	−.60
Truck driver ..	.46	−.31	−.37	.36	.02	−.02	−.49	−.21	.39
Warehouseman	−.45	−.05	.54	−.34	−.04	.10	.12	.38	−.15

[a] The largest value of r in each column is italicized.

Table 22. Correlations among Nine Final Homogeneous Keys and Thirteen Navy Keys for a Sample of 400 Navy Men in General

Key	H_{1b}	H_{2b}	H_{3b}	H_{4b}	H_{5b}	H_{6b}	H_{7b}	H_{9b}	H_{0b}
AD	−.16	−.31	−.59	.32	−.25	.17	−.63	−.44	.62
BM	.01	−.14	−.21	−.31	.31	.45	−.19	−.05	.12
CS	−.35	.17	.04	−.26	.86[a]	.05	.23	.11	−.39
CT	−.72	.24	.66	−.14	.00	−.38	.70	.47	−.53
DC	.22	−.20	−.20	−.38	−.05	.82	−.32	−.18	.28
EM	.57	−.17	−.41	.90	−.16	−.58	−.35	−.24	.31
ET	.03	.23	−.08	.60	−.02	−.72	.20	−.08	−.12
FC	.36	−.15	−.14	.79	−.20	−.59	−.17	−.18	.11
GM	.83	−.43	−.58	.38	−.25	.26	−.81	−.39	.69
HM	−.41	.91	−.06	−.36	.22	−.12	.34	.01	−.28
QM	−.63	.39	.34	−.32	.18	−.17	.70	.32	−.40
RD	−.05	−.10	.04	.53	.03	−.49	.33	.10	−.14
SK	−.79	.03	.91	−.48	.03	−.02	.47	.59	−.53

[a] The largest value of r in each column is italicized.

Characteristics of Homogeneous Keys

Since item content played no role in the development of the homogeneous keys, it is a matter of some interest to examine the nature of responses that clustered together. A description of these items for the final set of homogeneous keys follows.

H_{1b}: The items in this key relate primarily to mechanics, machine operation and design, or to home repairs of mechanical and simple electrical gadgets.

H_{2b}: The items in this key express interests in medical and hospital service activities and occupations or in doing medical, biological, or chemical research.

H_{3b}: Interests in general office clerical work and office machine operation, bookkeeping and accounting, and office management are indicated by the items scored on this key.

H_{4b}: These items deal with the maintenance, operation, and building of radio and other electronic equipment and with the repair and construction of electrical systems and devices.

H_{5b}: These items are concerned almost completely with interests in the preparation of food and menu planning.

H_{6b}: The content of the major cluster apparent in this key deals with carpentry and furniture-making. The remaining items (plus some in the above cluster) seem quite unrelated, although each selected item involves the rejection of an alternative that deals with electrical-electronic or with medical-chemical interests.

H_{7b}: Two clusters of content are indicated by these items. The largest deals with a variety of verbal activities while the other indicates interests in aesthetics. A few of the items express an interest in people; others seem related only in that they seem socially accepted, "highly thought of" activities.

H_{9b}: There seems to be no easily interpretable common theme indicated by these items, although it appears that high scores on this key reflect preference for "clean-hand" kinds of activities.

H_{0b}: The major cluster of items in this key reflects interests in athletics and other outdoor activities. A second set of interests deals with unskilled manual jobs and home repairs. The remainder seems to indicate a sort of compulsiveness or neatness about simple manual tasks. The alternatives to the keyed responses reflect aversions to feminine, indoor, verbal, and responsible complex activities.

A comparison of these nine homogeneous scales with the two sets of factors obtained by other investigators, cited earlier in this chapter, makes it clear that we have not developed a set of factorially simple scales. The descriptions of content likewise suggest complex structure. Factorial simplicity and scale homogeneity are not synonymous. The development of a limited number of dimensions for describing the vocational interests of individuals might have included procedures which would have yielded factorially simple scales; our procedures could not be expected to do so and were not intended to do so.

What we have done, however, is important to note. We have begun by looking only at the interrelationships of responses to a vocational interest inventory. From the study of correlations among responses we have developed scales which are made up of those responses which "go together." These scales turn out to have certain orderly relations to scales developed in an entirely different fashion. The import of this finding will be discussed in detail in succeeding chapters.

Use of Occupational and Homogeneous Keys in Classifying Men into Occupations

THE preceding chapters have reviewed the development of the Minnesota Vocational Interest Inventory, the administering of this inventory to large numbers of employed civilian workers in many occupational groups and to men in the various Navy rating groups, the development of empirical and homogeneous scoring keys, and the characteristics of these keys. This has permitted a limited appraisal of the effectiveness of empirical keys through comparison of the distributions of scores made by men in an occupational group with the scores made by a reference group or a men-in-general group; it has not permitted any evaluation of the empirical validity of homogeneous keys except by showing the way in which these keys correlate with empirical keys.

The effectiveness of keys in classifying men into occupational groups is much more difficult to evaluate for homogeneous than for empirical keys. Homogeneous keys are developed to be used in concert with other homogeneous keys. They are not intended to be used alone in the way empirical keys are used. The empirical key is, in a sense, the best key for a particular classification problem; it is the composite of those items which do the most effective job of differentiating between men in one group and men in another.

Any proper evaluation of a homogeneous key needs to examine the way in which it operates in combination with other homogeneous keys. This is the natural use of such keys, for they are designed to reflect the various di-

The Vocational Interests of Nonprofessional Men

mensions of responses that exist, and to yield a fairly complete summary of all responses made by an individual.

The statistic which has been used in earlier chapters to indicate the degree to which an empirical key is performing its function is the index of overlapping, in which the degree of separation between the distributions of scores of men in the criterion and reference groups is indicated by the area common to the two standardized distributions. The median percentage of overlap obtained with empirical keys is approximately 50 when we look at the original groups on which the keys were developed, and also about 50 when we look at the percentage of overlap of distributions of cross-validation samples. The use of the percentage of overlap permits us to make an estimation of the degree of separation between two groups without our estimate being influenced by the size of the sample involved and without this estimate varying appreciably from key to key because of differences in the amount of variability or number of items in different keys. This percentage of overlap, let us note, is a sole function of the difference between the two means, divided by the average of the two standard deviations.* This latter ratio is approximately 1.35 when the percentage of overlap is 50.

There is no easily comparable statistic to the percentage of overlap for the analyses we have made using combinations of homogeneous keys. The measure of differentiation which we have employed is the D^2 statistic of Mahalonobis (1949). This statistic is a measure of the generalized distance between two groups whose characteristics are being compared on a number of variables. The D^2 statistic (or D) has many characteristics in common with our statistic, the percentage of overlap. It is a measure of the degree of separation which is not affected by the size of the samples involved; it is not markedly influenced by the differences in the variabilities of the keys involved and likewise is not affected by the number of items in each one of the keys except as the number of items may affect the way in which that key operates. The value of D^2 thus is a pure number just as is the percentage of overlap. When the D^2 value is computed using only two groups, D is, in effect, the difference between the two means or the two composite means expressed in standard score terms. In a multivariate space the value of D is again expressed in standard score terms, except that we now are dealing

*When the two standard deviations are grossly different, this index fails to adjust for the relative size of the two groups; in most of our comparisons, differences are not great.

70

Use of Keys in Classifying Men into Occupations

with distance separating the position of one group from the position of the other, expressed in terms of variability, on several dimensions rather than one. It seems appropriate for us to assume that two groups who differ from each other on a given single key by one standard deviation would have the same overlapping of distributions as would occur for two groups whose mean values on a composite of keys differ by a generalized distance (D) of 1.0 with the single reservation that "overlap" is not the best descriptive term to use in the latter instances.

We might, then, compare combinations of homogeneous keys with single empirical keys by comparing D values with a similar index, such as that used to enter Tilton's tables, namely $M_1 - M_2/\frac{1}{2}$ $(\sigma_1 + \sigma_2)$. However, since the D^2 statistic is expressed in terms of within-group variances, it seems more appropriate to compare D and $M_1 - M_2/\sigma_1$ where σ_1 is the standard deviation of the distribution of scores made by members of the *criterion* group. (The reference group, being heterogeneous in content, would have a variance composed partly of within-group and partly of between-group variances.) Such comparisons are presented in Table 23. The comparison is possible for a group of nineteen Navy ratings for which empirical keys were developed and for which weighted combinations of homogeneous keys were computed. The computation of the D values was part of a much larger study completed by Norman (1957, 1960).

Table 23 should be read as follows. The weighted combination of homogeneous keys permits the separation of men in the Navy rating AD from Navy men in general not quite as well as the single AD empirical key will do, since the difference (D) for the former is 1.02 compared to the differences of 1.29 using the latter key with the original criterion group and 1.49 with the cross-validation group of AD's. The table generally shows that the amount of separation for the weighted combination of homogeneous keys is a bit smaller than that of the empirical keys, whether we look at the original criterion group or the cross-validation group. These differences, however, are not uniform. The HM group is identified better, for example, on the combination of homogeneous keys than it is with the best empirical key. This difference is large and noteworthy. Likewise the SK key, the CS key, and the RM key developed empirically do not do quite as well as the combinations of homogeneous keys.

It is interesting to note that those groups for which the homogeneous keys work best are those for rating groups quite different from the typical Navy activity. The classification of Navy men is most difficult for the very

71

The Vocational Interests of Nonprofessional Men

Table 23. Distances between Criterion and Reference Groups for Homogeneous and for Empirical Scoring Keys

Navy Group	Weighted Combination of Homogeneous Keys [a]	Single Empirical Key [b]	
		Original Group	Cross-Validation Group [c]
AD (aviation machinist's mate)	1.02	1.29	1.49
AT (aviation electronics technician)	1.63	1.69	2.08
BM (boatswain's mate)	0.93	1.25	
BT (boilerman)	0.68	0.90	
CS (commissaryman)	2.12	1.73	1.69
CT (communications technician)	1.24	1.40	
DC (damage controlman)	1.35	1.53	1.66
EM (electrician's mate)	1.14	1.58	1.18
EN (engineman)	0.87	1.39	1.68
ET (electronics technician)	1.57	2.02	1.99
FC (fire controlman)	1.23	1.24	1.48
GM (gunner's mate)	0.75	1.03	0.66; 1.16
HM (hospitalman)	2.52	1.49	1.55
MM (machinist's mate)	0.72	1.17	1.28
QM (quartermaster)	1.16	1.36	1.25
RD (radarman)	1.03	1.51	0.86
RM (radioman)	1.75	1.46	
SK (storekeeper)	1.71	1.48	
YN (yeoman)	1.59	1.54	1.59; 1.32

[a] D values.

[b] $(M_1 - M_2)/\sigma_1$; see the text.

[c] For GM and YN there were two cross-validation groups.

large proportion of persons who enter mechanical or technical activities. The fine distinctions employed in these rates make it difficult to develop keys that sort them out well. We are, perhaps, asking our homogeneous keys to do too refined a task in making this separation. Why the empirical keys should work when the homogeneous keys do not work as well, however, requires more of an explanation than the one just given.

One may have some reservations about the data of Table 23 because a D value seems to differ so much from the difference between means divided by one standard deviation. Some reassurance may be obtained in this regard by examination of the data in Table 24. These data were obtained from the analysis of a small sample of Navy rating groups which were being separated from each other by combinations of homogeneous keys and also by combinations of empirical keys. They permit us to compute the value of $(M_1 - M_2)/(\sigma_1 + \sigma_2)/2$ and to compare it with the value of D obtained in the analysis. Table 24 does not use the standard deviation of the criterion

72

Use of Keys in Classifying Men into Occupations

Table 24. Generalized Distances (D) Compared with Mean
Differences (z) between Four Navy Rating Groups

Navy Groups	D	z^a
ADL₁ Key		
AD and GM	0.71	0.70
AD and ET	2.07	2.00
AD and FC	1.47	1.43
ET and FC	0.59	0.59
ET and GM	1.53	1.39
FC and GM	0.77	0.79
H₁ₐ Key		
AD and GM	0.02	0.02
AD and ET	0.72	0.76
AD and FC	0.41	0.43
ET and FC	0.31	0.30
ET and GM	0.74	0.74
FC and GM	0.43	0.42

Source: Gee (1955).
[a] $z = (M_1 - M_2)/\frac{1}{2}(\sigma_1 + \sigma_2)$.

groups for a divisor but rather the average of the two standard deviations, since both groups are single occupational groups. It should be noted that the D values and the $(M_1 - M_2)/(\sigma_1 + \sigma_2)/2$ values are very close approximations to each other.

The same analysis which was the source for the data presented in Table 24 permits a direct comparison of D values using homogeneous or empirical keys. These values are shown in Table 25. The data come from two somewhat different studies, both, however, using the generalized distance function. One study, by Norman, used a total of 115 occupational groups. The other study, by Gee, used only 4 groups.

Table 25. Generalized Distances (D) between Four Navy Groups
for Combinations of Three Types of Keys

Navy Groups	Preliminary Homogeneous Keys[a]	Final Homogeneous Keys[b]	Shortened Empirical Keys[a]
AD and GM	0.59	1.10	1.34
AD and ET	1.88	2.01	2.96
AD and FC	1.56	1.76	2.32
ET and FC	0.81	0.73	1.05
ET and GM	1.73	2.04	2.63
FC and GM	1.28	1.61	1.83

[a] Data are from Gee (1955).
[b] Data are from Norman (1957).

73

The Vocational Interests of Nonprofessional Men

Table 25 presents the D values obtained with combinations of nine homogeneous keys (the keys being slightly different between the two studies) for the comparison of the four Navy rating groups with each other. Again there is considerable resemblance between the two sets of data, the values of D obtained by Norman being somewhat larger than those obtained by Gee. The relative values for pairs, however, are very close. It may be that the D values obtained by Norman are larger because the homogeneous keys had been improved, or because his use of a much larger number of groups resulted in an over-all within-group dispersion matrix that differed considerably from that obtained by Gee.

The Gee analysis provided an opportunity for comparison of the combination of homogeneous keys with a combination of empirical keys. Table 23 presented the comparison of the weighted combinations of homogeneous keys with a single empirical key. Table 25 supports the conclusion that the best combination of empirical keys is far superior to the best combination of homogeneous keys, the D values being of markedly greater magnitude when combinations of empirical keys are used.

A major issue in the use of homogeneous keys is the degree to which the single scores may be used without a weighting formula in order to get a composite. To what extent does an individual homogeneous key separate a group from men in general? Table 26 presents some data on this point for two Navy rating groups. These data were obtained from the analysis of the 115 occupational groups previously reported. It is not always the case that there is a single homogeneous key that is a good one for a particular group. For the aviation machinist's mates no single homogeneous key works well, and the composite fails to do a reasonably good job of separation. The value of 1.02 for the D between AD's and NMIG on a combination of homogeneous keys needs to be compared with the value of 1.29 for z which can be computed from Table 12 of Chapter 3. AD's are not well separated from the total Navy group in either instance.

The hospitalman group does have a homogeneous key that works better than some weighted composites. The H2 key places the reference group 1.74 standard deviations below the criterion group. The composite does even better, demonstrating the marked differences between the interests of men in the hospital group and those in the Navy at large.

The work of Norman with 115 occupational groups has been cited as the source for some of the comparative statistics presented earlier in this chapter. His primary objective was to determine the degree to which the use of

74

Use of Keys in Classifying Men into Occupations

Table 26. Effectiveness of Single Homogeneous Keys and a
Weighted Composite Score in Separating a Navy Rating
Group from Navy Men in General for Two
Navy Groups

Key	Navy Rating Group		Standard Distance from Mean of Navy Men in General [a]
	Mean	S.D.	
Aviation Machinist's Mates (N = 70)			
H1	15.57	4.47	+0.73
H2	4.34	3.53	−0.21
H3	3.13	3.26	−0.46
H4	8.13	3.80	−0.11
H5	3.94	2.55	−0.42
H6	7.69	3.52	+0.11
H7	3.73	3.02	−0.31
H8	3.67	2.29	−0.46
H9	9.11	2.05	+0.27
Weighted composite			1.02
Hospitalmen (N = 70)			
H1	4.99	4.73	−1.55
H2	14.86	5.47	+1.74
H3	5.47	4.20	+0.20
H4	3.93	3.63	−1.27
H5	6.00	3.34	+0.29
H6	6.90	3.16	−0.10
H7	7.67	3.95	+0.75
H8	4.81	2.11	+0.04
H9	7.11	2.95	−0.49
Weighted composite			2.52

[a] All values are $(M_1 - M_2)/\sigma_1$ except the value for the weighted composite, which is the generalized distance (D).

the generalized distance function with a set of nine homogeneous keys for an interest inventory would permit the sorting of occupational groups into meaningful clusters or job families. The use of a small number of keys with a large number of occupational groups also yields some insights into the way in which these keys describe the meaningful dimensions of vocational interests.

Table 27 presents Norman's findings in the clusters which seemed to provide the best sorting of groups. Groups listed in the left-hand column are considered to belong in clusters; those in the right-hand column are listed next to the cluster to which they are closest but are considered not to

Table 27. Clusters, Cumulative Average Intracluster and Extracluster Distances, and Cluster Separability Indexes, Together with Proximal Nonclustered Groups and Their Average Distances to the Cluster

NOTE: The cumulative average intracluster (D_I) and extracluster (D_E) and separability indexes ($SE = D_I/D_E$) are given for the composite of all groups included in the cluster. That is, in cluster C_2, for example, the cumulative average intracluster for the tradeswoman-in-general and female retail sales clerk groups is .66; for these groups and the secretary and office clerk group it is 1.02; etc. When a group seemed not to fall reasonably into any cluster, the average distances from all clusters in its vicinity were calculated and the group was appended to the cluster from which it had the smallest average distance. Such groups are listed in the table as "Proximal Nonclustered Groups" and the final column gives their average D value from the associated cluster (D_C). For clusters of three or more groups, the one closest to the weighted center of the cluster (i.e., whose average distance from the others in the cluster is minimal) is indicated by an asterisk. A reference group is indicated by (R).

Cluster	Clustered Groups	Ave. D_I	Ave. D_E	SI	Proximal Nonclustered Groups	Ave. D_C
C_1	Beauty culture					
	Dressmaking	.75	3.03	.25		
C_2	Tradeswoman in general (R)				SLA student, female (R)	2.07
	Retail sales clerk, female *	.66	2.95	.22		
	Secretary and office clerk	1.02	2.99	.34		
	IBM operator, female	1.15	2.87	.40		
C_3	Aviation storekeeper				Teleman	1.16
	Storekeeper*	.53	2.18	.24		
	Yeoman	.65	2.16	.30		
	Personnel man	.74	2.21	.33		
	Disbursing clerk	.82	2.33	.35		
C_4	Hospital corpsman				Psychiatric aide	1.15
	Dental technician	.71	2.64	.27		
C_5	Aviation photographer's mate				Musician	1.12
					SLA student, male (R)	1.37
	Photographer's mate	.82	2.04	.40	Journalist	1.41
C_6	Salesperson				Parachute rigger	1.04
	Retail sales clerk, male	.57	1.56	.37	IBM operator, male	1.33
C_7	Aerographer's mate				Quartermaster	1.09
	New car salesman	.72	1.86	.36		
C_8	Milk wagon driver				Machine accountant	1.02
	Torpedoman's mate*	.36	1.42	.25		
	Ship's serviceman	.57	1.45	.39		
	Warehouseman	.63	1.43	.44		
C_9	Washington High School freshman				Sonarman	.72
					Baker wagon driver	.80
	Washington High School sophomore	.39	1.37	.28	Submariner student in general (R)	.88

76

Table 27—continued

Clus-ter	Clustered Groups	Ave. D_I	Ave. D_E	SI	Proximal Nonclustered Groups	Ave. D_C
	Washington High School junior	.52	1.38	.38	Air controlman	.93
					Bakery company employee (R)	1.03
	Washington High School senior	.54	1.41	.38	Steward	1.63
	Employment office in general (R)	.55	1.41	.39		
	Shipping and stock clerk	.59	1.42	.42		
C_{10}	Plumbing*				Baker	.78
	Aviation ordnanceman	.31	1.31	.24	Printing	.82
	Aviation boatswain's mate	.35	1.32	.27	Drafting, architectural	.89
	Navy man in general (R)	.43	1.31	.33	Confectioner	1.01
	Drafting, mechanical	.48	1.32	.36	Commissaryman	2.14
C_{11}	Automobile mechanics					
	Tool and die making	.63	1.54	.41		
	Vocational high school (R)	.71	1.50	.47		
C_{12}	Auto paint and body					
	Masonry	.73	1.57	.46		
C_{13}	Printer					
	Engineering student (R)	.74	1.51	.49		
C_{14}	Pressman				Transformer winder	.72
	Foreman (R)	.40	1.44	.28	Lithographer	.89
C_{15}	Machinist				Aviation structural mechanic	1.07
	Sheet metal worker	.27	1.60	.17	Refrigeration serviceman	1.14
	Machinery repairman	.34	1.60	.21		
	Aviation machinist's mate	.36	1.59	.23		
	Engineman*	.41	1.57	.26		
	Plumber	.45	1.59	.28		
	Steam fitter	.47	1.61	.29		
	Metalsmith	.50	1.61	.31		
	Utilities man	.52	1.62	.32		
	Machinist's mate	.54	1.61	.34		
	Tradesman in general (R)	.55	1.60	.34		
	Boilerman	.56	1.59	.35		
	Plumbing and pipe fitting	.57	1.59	.36		
	Machine operator (R)	.58	1.60	.36		
	Driver	.59	1.60	.37		
	Truck mechanic	.62	1.62	.38		
	Dunwoody trade school (R)	.63	1.63	.39		
	Pipe fitter	.64	1.64	.39		
	Machine shop	.66	1.66	.40		
	Pipe fitter	.68	1.68	.40		
	Gunner's mate	.69	1.68	.41		
	Truck driver	.70	1.69	.41		
	Mechanic	.71	1.69	.42		
	Machine shop	.72	1.70	.42		
C_{16}	Boatswain's mate					
	Sheet metal worker	.57	1.51	.38		

Table 27—continued

Cluster	Clustered Groups	Ave. D_I	Ave. D_E	SI	Proximal Nonclustered Groups	Ave. D_C
C_{17}	Painter and decorator					
	Plasterer	.57	1.47	.39		
C_{18}	Builder				Cement finisher	.76
	Damage controlman	.43	1.91	.23		
	Carpenter	.50	1.92	.26		
	Carpentry	.57	1.88	.30		
	Carpentry and cabinet making	.63	1.90	.33		
C_{19}	Aviation electronics technician					
	Electronics technician	.36	2.00	.18		
	Interior communication technician	.56	2.00	.28		
	Electrician's mate	.62	1.91	.32		
	Fire controlman	.64	1.89	.34		
	Aviation electrician's mate	.66	1.91	.35		
	Electrician	.69	1.94	.36		
	Electrical	.72	1.98	.36		
	Construction electrician's mate	.76	2.00	.38		
	Radio, television, electronics	.79	2.04	.39		
C_{20}	Radioman					
	Communications technician*	.72	1.99	.36		
	Radarman	.75	1.88	.40		

belong in the cluster in the same sense as are the groups on the left. (Persons who find these D values of interest may profitably refer to Norman's thesis, which lists each of the 6555 ($\frac{1}{2}(115 \times 114)$) pairwise D values for the 115 groups.)

The nature of clusters is often sensible and meaningful, attesting to the efficacy of the homogeneous keys in reflecting differences between groups as we generally understand them. Cluster 3, for example, is the familiar clerical group with Cluster 2 being a slight modification of it. Clusters 4, 5, and 6 seem to fit our knowledge of these groups, with Cluster 7 being a bit anomalous. Clusters 15 and 19 are distressing, however, since each lumps together more groups, and more diverse groups, than we would like. For purposes of improving the use of these keys in classifying or counseling, Cluster 15 ought to be broken into two or three or four groups. Cluster 19 should split to yield an electronic and an electrical group. Thus the data of this table suggest some deficiencies in the battery of homogeneous keys being used.

Use of Keys in Classifying Men into Occupations

A comparable analysis of the 115 occupational groups in which a set of empirical keys is used rather than homogeneous keys is an obvious next step. This work has not yet been done. It is possible, however, to predict from data now available that the average distances between clusters will be greater when empirical keys are used, and that clusters like 15 and 17 may be broken into subgroups. It is not possible, of course, to make predictions with certainty about the way in which occupations will cluster in such a new analysis. Since we have already noted the high correlations between certain empirical and certain homogeneous keys, it seems reasonable to assume, however, that great changes will not occur.

Even though the homogeneous keys do not separate groups as well as empirical keys, the degree of separation is still substantial. In Table 27 the average D value between clusters is usually larger than 1.5. Any investigator who separates criterion groups by an amount equal to 1.5 standard deviations is ordinarily delighted with his findings. These differences are large enough to suggest the feasibility of their use with individuals, in addition to establishing their obvious value for drawing inferences about the structure of vocational interests. And we can assume that they would be even larger if empirical keys were used.

Earlier in the chapter attention was directed to the superiority of combinations of homogeneous keys over empirical keys for several Navy rating groups. These groups fall in Clusters 3, 4, and 20. (The commissaryman group stands alone, being 2.14 units away from the nearest cluster.) These clusters again include essentially nonmechanical, nontechnical groups, and show the same relatively greater distance from other clusters that was observed in the earlier analysis.

These findings suggest that empirical keys may seem quite a bit superior to our best combinations of homogeneous keys not because such keys are inherently better, but because our set of homogeneous keys fails to tap certain dimensions of interest. Especially among those occupations which are all "mechanical" there probably needs to be a separation of interests relating to such diverse areas as (1) principles of machine function, perhaps including trouble shooting, (2) bench machine work, including tool and die making and fabrication of parts, (3) routine disassembly, cleaning, and reassembly, (4) machine operation and routine maintenance, (5) general handyman activities, and (6) assembly of parts, either on a routine or a "custom-built" basis. Perhaps the procedures employed in developing homogeneous keys are insufficiently refined to permit such scales to emerge;

The Vocational Interests of Nonprofessional Men

or perhaps these interests are not sufficiently overrepresented in the item pool to permit them to emerge as separate scales. (The adequacy of empirical keys in this domain discounts the likelihood of the latter suggestion being correct.) A still further possibility is that the standards set for homogeneity within scales prevent the use of certain items which would achieve the separations desired. At any rate, exploration of these points in further studies seems to be required.

Another approach to the practical problem of developing an appropriate set of interest measures for an inventory is suggested by the earlier evidence on high correlations between certain empirical and homogeneous keys. If these correlations are this high, we might well preserve the desirable psychometric qualities which both types of keys provide. Our later evidence on ability to separate groups is generally favorable to the use of empirical rather than homogeneous keys. But to use certain empirical keys is not to lose the orderliness of homogeneous keys if the empirical keys are selected because of their near identity to homogeneous keys, and if we are willing to use only a small number of such keys.

The choice of an empirical key rather than a homogeneous one is not hard to defend in terms of validity. The examples in the accompanying tabulation suffice as support.

	Criterion Group		Reference Group		Percent-age of Overlap
	Mean	S.D.	Mean	S.D.	
HM					
Empirical key	25.1	17.2	−0.6	12.3	38
Best homogeneous key	14.86	5.61	5.08	5.08	36
ET					
Empirical key	19.4	8.6	2.0	10.2	35
Best homogeneous key	12.61	3.82	8.53	4.74	63
CS					
Empirical key	7.4	11.4	−12.3	9.4	34
Best homogeneous key	11.44	4.81	5.02	3.84	46
Machinist					
Empirical key	22.8	7.0	10.5	8.6	43
Best homogeneous key	16.60	4.42	14.74	5.49	85
Mechanic					
Empirical key	40.3	8.6	27.7	12.7	55
Best homogeneous key	17.96	3.63	14.74	5.49	72
Electrician					
Empirical key	29.6	6.2	13.7	8.5	28
Best homogeneous key	14.20	3.04	8.94	4.03	46

This choice would not necessarily mean that a large number of empirical keys would be required, or that a new key would have to be developed for each new occupation. Our study of homogeneous keys — of their usefulness in identifying basic dimensions, and of their deficiencies in classification — suggests that the selection of those empirical keys highly correlated with homogeneous keys, plus one, two, or three additional keys in the mechanical areas, would provide an adequate scoring system for the MVII. Furthermore, it seems likely that such a system would come close to being a "closed system," since we would expect that little usable item variance would remain untapped in the inventory, and hence that new keys would not be required. Such a prediction is, of course, rash. But the evidence on the minimal number of scoring keys needed from which this prediction derives is, after all, much greater than is ordinarily available for most published tests.

✦ 6 ✦

Predicting Achievement and Choice
of Specialty

THE effectiveness of interest inventory scoring keys in differentiating between employed groups has been amply illustrated in the preceding chapters. These data suggest that scores on interest inventories may be used to advantage in suggesting appropriate areas of work for persons facing problems of occupational choice. We might even, if we are willing to go considerably beyond the data presented thus far, use these scores as estimates of the degree to which a person would like a given occupation, or be motivated to achieve in a given area of study.

The earlier work of Strong with his Vocational Interest Blank encourages some generalization. His monumental follow-up study (1955) of Stanford University students eighteen years after they had completed his blank presents convincing evidence of the great stability of his interest scores over long time intervals, and of their usefulness in predicting persistence in an occupation.

No data comparable in scope to that available for the Strong blank exist for the Minnesota Vocational Interest Inventory. A number of studies have been completed, however, which suggest that it yields scores which have merit for predictive as well as classification purposes. These data complement those obtained with the Strong blank, since they test the use of measured interests in different settings from those in which the Strong blank is generally used.

Predicting Achievement and Choice of Specialty

MEASURED INTERESTS AND ACHIEVEMENT
IN SCHOOL AND ON THE JOB

In research undertaken to investigate specifically the relationships among measured interests, aptitudes, and achievement as indicated by marks in Navy schools and by ratings of supervisors, three samples of students were studied: 354 students at the Class "A" AT School at Memphis, 464 students from the Class "A" AD School at Memphis, and 547 students from the Class "A" School for ET's at Great Lakes. The procedures followed in data collection and analysis were essentially the same for the three groups and may be described as follows.

The samples were made up of the men from four or five entire classes in each of the separate schools who received their training between 1950 and 1952. The schools in which the men were enrolled were those which prepare recruits for entering specific navy ratings. Excepting less than 1 per cent of each sample, the men came to the schools directly from recruit training. All had taken the Navy Basic Test Battery (BTB) including the following aptitude tests: Navy General Classification Test (GCT), Arithmetical Reasoning Test (ARI), and Mechanical Aptitude Test (MAT). For the two Navy aviation student groups, scores on the Clerical Aptitude Test (CLER) were also available. The Navy Vocational Interest Inventory was administered during the course of training in each of the schools. In as much as achievement was measured by the final numerical grades in the technical school training courses, only those men are included in the samples who successfully completed the courses.

Multiple regression methods were used to gain insight into relationships between interest and ability measures as they are combined in a linear fashion to predict school grade achievement. In order to gain further insight into the manner in which a motivational variable such as interest functions in an achievement setting of this kind, analysis of each sample includes computation of the correlation of interest with achievement when general ability is held constant at various levels. For the ET sample the correlations of arithmetical reasoning and mechanical aptitude with achievement when general ability is held constant were also computed.

Table 28, which shows the means and standard deviations of each of the three samples on the variables employed in the studies, highlights the fact that we are not dealing with groups that are representative of the average Navy enlisted man. However, since the Navy Basic Test Battery was originally standardized so as to approximate the conditions that would exist un-

The Vocational Interests of Nonprofessional Men

Table 28. Means and Standard Deviations of Navy Aviation Technical
School Students on Ability Measures

Measure	AT Students (N = 354)		AD Students (N = 461)		ET Students (N = 547)	
	Mean	S.D.	Mean	S.D.	Mean	S.D.
GCT	63.66	5.16	59.46	5.44	65.35	4.77
ARI	62.30	5.19	59.98	5.54	63.06	6.25
MAT	58.51	7.02	54.43	7.57	60.65	6.31
CLER	55.33	7.21	53.26	7.43		

der full mobilization, the means set at 50 and the standard deviations at 10 are probably not representative of the present total Navy complement either. While we do not know the means and standard deviations of the present total Navy complement, we believe that the range of abilities is somewhat restricted in our samples. However, knowledge of differential recruitment policies strongly suggests that this restriction is less severe than it would be under conditions of full mobilization.

Electronics Technicians. The interest scores for this group are based on one of the revised scoring keys for the Navy Vocational Interest Inventory. Items for this "ET" key were selected on the basis of a high or moderately high percentage difference in response between a criterion group of rated electronics technicians and a reference group of Navy men in general (high validity index), and on the basis of low correlation with the total score. The overlapping of the original ET group with Navy men in general was only 35 per cent (see Table 34). When the key was cross-validated using another sample of rated ET's, the overlapping was practically the same (36 per cent). The mean of the cross-validation sample of ET's on this key was 19.5 and the standard deviation 8.8. The present sample of students compares favorably with rated ET's in their measured interests, having a mean score of 16.8 with a standard deviation of 9.1.

Table 29 shows a matrix of intercorrelations of the variables used to predict achievement in the Navy Electronics Technician Technical School. The separate correlations of each variable with the criterion, β coefficients, and significance data are also given. The β coefficients, which are standard partial regression coefficients, would in a prediction equation be used with standard scores and are, therefore, directly comparable.

For this group the interest measure accounts for more of the variation in school grades than does any one of the measures of general and special ability; in fact, the interest inventory score accounts for more independent

Predicting Achievement and Choice of Specialty

Table 29. Correlation Matrix and β Coefficients for Prediction of Achievement in Navy Electronics Technician School (N = 547 ET School Students)

| | Correlation Matrix | | | | | |
Measure	ARI	MAT	Interest	School Grade	β Coefficient	b/SE_b
GCT	.24***	.21***	.03	.19***	.1272	3.06**
ARI		.00	.00	.14***	.1137	2.80**
MAT			.01	.18***	.1499	3.72**
Interest				.30***	.2994	7.60**

** Significant at the .01 level.
*** Significant at the .001 level.

criterion variance than the sum of GCT, ARI, MAT. The multiple correlation of the four combined predictor variables with the criterion of achievement is .40. The F ratio is 25.67, which is significant beyond the .001 level.

An attempt was made further to clarify the role of an interest variable in the prediction of achievement by observing the correlations between these two variables when general ability is held constant at various levels. The results are given in Table 30.

Explicitly limiting the range of general ability appears to bring about a variable amount of incidental limitation in the ranges of the interest and achievement variables with whose correlation we are concerned. As might be expected, since GCT and achievement are significantly correlated over the entire range of ability, the effect on achievement of holding general ability constant is most marked at the higher levels. When general ability is very high (70 or above), an upward shift in mean achievement score occurs

Table 30. Means, Standard Deviations, and Correlations between Interests and Achievement at Various Levels of General Ability for an Electronics Technician Sample

GCT Level	No.	r between Interest and Achievement	Interest Scores		Achievement Scores	
			Mean	S.D.	Mean	S.D.
70 and above	106	.13	17.83	8.21	76.03	5.59
67–69	131	.34**	16.73	8.41	74.42	5.63
64–66	138	.28**	15.53	9.73	72.17	5.58
61–63	81	.47**	17.84	10.40	73.78	6.16
60 and below	91	.34**	16.46	8.71	72.37	5.64
All	547	.30**	16.76	9.11	73.71	5.87

** Significant at the .01 level.

85

The Vocational Interests of Nonprofessional Men

as well as a decrease in standard deviation. The mean score on the interest variable shifts proportionally less than, but in the same direction as, the mean achievement score.

There is maximum variability of both interest and achievement at a GCT level which is just under the mean for this group (M = 65.35). Here, holding constant general ability has allowed a correlation of interest with achievement to emerge, and the correlation at .47 is fairly high. At all other GCT levels, significant but smaller correlations are obtained.

Assuming that the relationship between general ability and arithmetical aptitude varies at different levels of ability, we would expect that where that relationship was strongest, the incidental restriction of the standard deviation of the arithmetical distribution would be greatest. It is at these levels of ability, however (GCT scores from 61 to 63 and 64 to 66), that significant correlations of arithmetical aptitude with achievement are obtained (see Table 31). The only correlation of mechanical aptitude with achievement that approaches significance when general ability is held constant is that at the 61–63 general ability level.

Aviation Electronics Technicians and Electronicsmen. This group was tested and scored on the Navy Vocational Interest Inventory before refinements in item selection had been applied to the scoring keys. The interest key used on this group was one for which items were selected only on the basis of percentage difference in response between rated aviation electronics technicians and a reference group of civilian tradesmen in general. The student group compares well with the rated criterion group on which the

Table 31. Means, Standard Deviations, and Correlations of Arithmetical and Mechanical Aptitudes with Achievement at Various Levels of General Ability for an Electronics Technician Sample

		r		ARI		MAT	
GCT Level	No.	ARI and Achieve-ment	MAT and Achieve-ment	Mean	S.D.	Mean	S.D.
70 and above .	106	.07	.03	65.79	8.05	62.39	6.03
67–69	131	.08	.12	63.51	5.59	61.22	6.57
64–66	138	.21*	.07	61.93	3.84	60.13	6.24
61–63	81	.24*	.19	62.57	4.82	60.65	5.48
60 and below .	91	−.02	.10	61.38	7.57	58.59	6.32
All	547	.14**	.18**	63.06	6.25	60.65	6.31

* Significant at the .05 level.
** Significant at the .01 level.

86

Predicting Achievement and Choice of Specialty

key is based, but it is expected that the refined AT key would be more effective than the one used in this study.

The intercorrelation matrix and related data for this group are shown in Table 32. For this group a measure of clerical aptitude was also available, but made no significant contribution to the regression equation and was accordingly dropped. With the exception of the GCT and ARI test, none of the remaining predictor variables were significantly correlated, nor were their separate correlations with the criterion significantly different from one another. This set of conditions results in coefficients which do not differ significantly and we find measured interest, GCT, MAT, and ARI scores

Table 32. Correlation Matrix and β Coefficients for Prediction of Achievement in Navy Aviation Electronics Technician and Electronicsmen School (N = 354 AT School Students)

Test	ARI	MAT	CLER	NVII	School Grade	β Coefficient [a]	b/SE_b
GCT	.14	.09	−.03	.05	.25***	.1846	3.81***
ARI		−.02	.21	.08	.30***	.2695	5.36***
MAT			−.17	−.07	.23***	.2355	4.86***
CLER				−.05	.01		
NVII					.24***	.2279	4.74***

*** Significant at the .001 level.

[a] These are the final standard partial regression coefficients arrived at after removal of the Clerical Aptitude Test from the regression equation.

Table 33. Means, Standard Deviations, and Correlations between Interest and Achievement for Aviation Electronics Technicians and Electronicsmen When General Ability Is Held Constant at Various Levels

GCT Level	No.	r between NVII and Achievement	Interest Scores Mean	S.D.	Achievement Scores Mean	S.D.
69 and above	72	.21	26.25	12.50	78.00	4.56
66–68	69	.31**	24.45	13.80	75.34	4.98
63–65	72	.10	25.90	13.85	75.92	4.13
60–62	64	.26*	25.55	15.75	74.74	4.52
57–59	42	.16	19.00	12.50	73.78	3.64
56 and below	35	−.05	23.15	14.30	74.50	4.46
All	354	.21**	24.95	14.00	75.60	4.64

Source: Kurz (1951).
* Significant at the .05 level.
** Significant at the .01 level.

The Vocational Interests of Nonprofessional Men

accounting for approximately equivalent amounts of variance in Aviation Electronics Technical School grades.

The multiple correlation coefficient resulting from linear combination of the four effective variables is .48. The F ratio is 26.20, which is significant beyond the .001 level of significance.

The relationships between interest and achievement when general ability is held constant are shown in Table 33.* These data do not offer as consistent a picture of relationships between interest and achievement as was the case with the electronics technician group. Possibly the small numbers in the subsamples are partially responsible. It appears here that except at the lowest level of ability significant positive correlations are obtained between interests and achievement.

Aviation Machinist's Mates. The interests of this group, like the AT sample, were scored on a key whose items were selected only on the basis of percentage difference in response between a criterion group of rated Navy men and a reference group of civilian tradesmen in general. Here too it is believed that the later refined keys would be more effective.

The multiple correlation results for this group are given in Table 34. In this case we find that MAT, measured interest, and GCT account for nearly all the predictable variance. Though all the partial regression coefficients are significant at the .001 level, MAT, which correlates substantially with the other two effective variables, is significantly more heavily weighted. The multiple correlation coefficient for this group is .52, using only three variables, and the F ratio is 56.87, significant at the .001 level.

Table 34. Correlation Matrix and β Coefficients for Prediction of Achievement in Navy Aviation Machinist's Mate School (N = 461 AD School Students)

Test	ARI	MAT	CLER	NVII	School Grade	β Coefficient [a]	b/SE_b
GCT	.12	.23	−.02	.04	.24***	.1463	3.59***
ARI		.07	.32	.00	.10*		
MAT			−.12	.32	.47***	.3754	8.74***
CLER				−.05	−.10*		
NVII					.31***	.1835	4.38***

* Significant at the .05 level.   *** Significant at the .001 level.
[a] Standard partial regression coefficients after removal of the arithmetical and clerical tests.

* All the data used in the analysis of aviation electronics technicians and aviation machinists were collected by Lloyd Allen Kurz (1951).

Predicting Achievement and Choice of Specialty

An incidental development, which may be of interest for other multiple regression studies of groups involved in activities of a mechanical nature, arose in the analysis of this group. In the original solution of the normal equations — in which all five of the variables were included — the coefficient for arithmetical aptitude was significant at the .05 level. When, however, the clerical aptitude test, which correlated .32 with arithmetic and −.10 with the achievement criterion, was removed from the regression equation because of its lack of significance, a reduction in significance level of the arithmetic test was simultaneously effected. The clerical test had apparently acted as a suppressor variable which allowed the arithmetic test to make an effective contribution. The combined effect of these two variables is not, in this instance, sufficient to warrant their retention in the multiple regression equation (R changes from .525 to .517 with their removal); the possibility of the use of clerical aptitude as a suppressor variable in the prediction of mechanical types of achievement is suggested.

The effect on the relationship between interest and achievement when general ability is held constant is presented in Table 35. As with the electronics technician group, significant correlations with achievement are found at nearly every level of ability. The correlation of .62 at the 60–62 GCT level suggests that when learning ability is just adequate, the motivational aspects of interests may play an important role in school achievement.

Table 35. Means, Standard Deviations, and Correlations between Interest and Achievement for Aviation Machinist's Mates When General Ability Is Held Constant at Various Levels.

GCT Level	No.	r between NVII and Achievement	NVII Scores Mean	S.D.	Achievement Scores Mean	S.D.
66 and above	67	.41**	10.40	7.02	79.24	5.32
63–65	62	.22	10.18	6.88	77.04	5.01
60–62	119	.62**	9.46	6.88	76.08	4.62
57–59	101	.29**	10.58	5.86	75.43	5.16
54–56	52	.32*	10.42	6.58	75.04	5.22
51–53	38	.41**	7.14	6.36	75.18	6.14
50 and below	25	−.01	11.06	5.64	74.10	5.94
All	464	.31**	9.92	6.68	76.10	5.40

Source: Kurz (1951).
* Significant at the .05 level.
** Significant at the .01 level.

The Vocational Interests of Nonprofessional Men

Tabulating Equipment Operators. An attempt to predict the proficiency ratings received by tabulating machine operators was made by Schenkel as his Ph.D. dissertation (1953). After he administered the Minnesota Vocational Interest Inventory to his sample, we developed from his data a scoring key for tabulating equipment operators; the Minnesota State Employment Service cooperated in the study by supplying the General Aptitude Test Battery, and administering and scoring it. Tabulator operators from 35 firms in Minneapolis and St. Paul were used in the study; 138 operators were employed on IBM equipment, 31 on Remington Rand; 114 were men, 55 were women.

An indication of the nature of the sample studied and of the differences between men and women operators on the several variables used may be obtained by examination of Table 36.

The analysis of interrelationships was based on the total group, men and women combined, even though on several of the variables significant and substantial sex differences were observed. In the work done to attempt the prediction of the criterion ratings with the tests available, a profile analysis method of the sort generally used by the U.S. Employment Service was adopted. The first step was an examination of the criterion ratings, which, upon analysis, were found to have a reliability of .82. The next step, deter-

Table 36. Means and Standard Deviations of Male and Female Tabulating Equipment Operators on Various Measures

Variable	Men (N = 114)		Women (N = 55)	
	Mean	S.D.	Mean	S.D.
GATB tests				
General Learning Aptitude ...	124.2	15.0	112.8	13.6
Verbal Aptitude	116.5	15.8	110.0	16.2
Numerical Aptitude	121.4	14.9	110.2	15.8
Space Perception	120.6	19.2	114.4	15.9
Form Perception	116.4	15.9	118.9	15.8
Clerical Aptitude	110.9	15.6	116.8	15.7
Aiming	103.6	14.8	103.9	13.9
Motor Speed	103.9	16.1	108.6	15.3
Finger Dexterity	105.9	18.6	108.6	17.1
Manual Dexterity	98.7	19.7	99.4	18.2
MVII	44.2	14.8	40.9	10.3
Proficiency criterion	20.0	5.6	17.9	5.2
Hoppock Job Satisfaction Blank No. 12.................	68.0	12.0	73.4	10.0
Miller-Remmers Attitude towards a Vocation Scale	32.0	7.3	33.3	8.5

Source: Schenkel (1953).

mining the correlation between each variable and these ratings, produced the results shown in Table 37.

It will be seen that there are no high validities, although several are significantly greater than zero. Profiles developed using various procedures failed consistently to include the vocational interest inventory score as one of the more useful predictors. Some basis for this failure may be observed in the interrelationships between variables as shown in Table 38. While the interest score does relate to proficiency, it relates, in this sample, even more to the aptitude measures which do the better job of predicting the proficiency criterion.

Table 37. Correlations of Aptitude Test Scores and MVII Scores
with the Proficiency Criterion for Tabulating Equipment
Operators (N = 169)

Variable	r
GATB tests	
General Learning Aptitude	.30**
Verbal Aptitude	.24**
Numerical Aptitude	.32**
Space Perception	.13
Form Perception	−.01
Clerical Aptitude	.18*
Aiming	.12
Motor Speed	.08
Finger Dexterity	.15*
Manual Dexterity	.04
MVII	.18*

Source: Schenkel (1953).
 * Significantly greater than zero at the .05 level.
 ** Significantly greater than zero at the .01 level.

Table 38. Correlations between Variables for Tabulating
Equipment Operators (N = 169)

Variable	Aptitude			Proficiency Rating	MVII	Hoppock	Miller-Remmers
	General	Numerical	Finger Dexterity				
Proficiency rating	.30	.32	.15		.18	.13	.21
MVII	.16	.36	−.01	.18*		.07	.22
Hoppock	−.09	−.06	.08	.13	.07		.33
Miller-Remmers	.14	.10	.01	.21**	.22	.33	

Source: Schenkel (1953).
 * Significant at the .05 level.
 ** Significant at the .01 level.

The Vocational Interests of Nonprofessional Men

The results of this study would thus suggest that interest inventory scores do not relate markedly to measures of on-the-job performance. This conclusion is not entirely warranted, however, since this study represents only a cross section of persons employed in a given occupation, and yields no great insight into processes of job selection, job tryout and change, and eventual satisfaction in a vocation. When only those persons are studied who have been employed and retained, and who have been willing to remain on a particular job, it is difficult to determine to what extent the relationships between variables observed within this sample describe the process by which these persons became eligible to be included in the sample. This is a particularly important problem in interest measurement, since the processes by which an occupational group is selected or changes in its interests in such a way as to make possible the development of keys of the sort we find are only poorly understood.

MEASURED INTERESTS AND JOB SATISFACTION

Relatively few data have been collected on the relationship of measured interests to job satisfaction, although this relationship is usually assumed to be high.

Strong in his monumental program of research with the Vocational Interest Blank has demonstrated long-term reliabilities of his scoring keys for professional groups and has shown substantial relationships between persistence in an occupation and the relevant scores on his blank.

One small bit of evidence on this relationship was obtained by Perry (1935) as a by-product of his work comparing forced-choice and Like-Indifferent-Dislike modes of responding to Navy Vocational Interest Inventory items. These data were obtained with a sample of yeomen enrolled in Class "C" schools. "Satisfaction" was measured rather crudely in terms of responses to a single item, "Would you select any other Navy rate in preference to this one?" Mean scores of those choosing the same or different ratings are given in Table 39 for the yeomen key of the interest inven-

Table 39. Scores on the Yeoman Key for Satisfied and Dissatisfied Yeomen

Response	No.	Mean	S.D.	Mean Difference	t
"Choose same rate"	85	32.0	34.0	21.7	3.40**
"Choose different rate"	50	10.3	36.8		

Source: Perry (1953).

** Significant at the .01 level.

92

tory. The satisfied group obtained significantly higher scores on this key than did the dissatisfied group. Further, those who were satisfied scored higher on the yeomen's key than did the criterion groups used in developing the key, suggesting that a satisfied group is a more valid group on which to develop keys. These findings suggest that the selection of persons with high scores on a given key will result in a higher proportion of satisfaction with the rating than is obtained when interest measures are not used.

MEASURED INTERESTS AND LATER CHOICE OF SPECIALTY

If the use of interest measures is intended to aid in occupational choice, it should be expected that choices of areas of work would be less appropriate when such measures are not used than when they are. It should also follow that even when such measures are not available at the time of choice, there should be some similarity between choices and those characteristics of the individual which interest measures estimate. The first of these two expectations is almost impossible to test, although some indirect evidences exist. The second expectation can be tested and has been in the study reported below.

Most studies of the relation between job choice and measured interests suffer from a contamination of the criterion by the test, since most of the time the interest scores are known at the time of counseling and occupational choice and are used in this process. A situation in which interest inventory responses were obtained from a large number of Navy airmen provided an opportunity to obtain follow-up data without this defect, since the inventories were not used in counseling and in fact were not scored until after the airmen had moved on to school or other assignments.

The sample population used in this study* consisted of 1971 Navy airmen recruits who attended Class "A" schools at Norman, Oklahoma, in 1954. Navy Basic Test Battery scores were available for all these men, including scores on the GCT, ARI, MAT, and CLER. Scores on these four tests are reported as Navy standard scores. During the first week of aviation training, these same men were given the Navy Vocational Interest Inventory.

Since this study aimed to appraise the classification process in Naval Air Technical Training, it would have been preferable had no test results been used in making assignments to schools. This was not the case, however,

---

* The succeeding sections draw heavily on the work of Dr. Diane R. Albitz. For a more complete report of this work, see Albitz (1958).

The Vocational Interests of Nonprofessional Men

since the counselors who assisted recruits in determining their preferences for Class "A" school assignments had knowledge of their BTB scores. However, as stated above, scores on the NVII were not available until after the recruits had been assigned to Class "A" school billets.*

Since one of the aims of the present study was to try to classify aviation recruits into a rating where they would have the greatest likelihood of resembling members of that group, empirical keys seemed more appropriate to use than homogeneous keys. On an intuitive basis it seemed there were at least several empirical keys that could differentiate the interests of men in the various Naval aviation ratings from Navy men in general: the BM key for aviation boatswain's mates, the AD key for aviation machinist's mates, the EM key for aviation electrician's mates, the SK key for aviation storekeepers, and the AT key for aviation electronics technicians. In order to get some concrete idea of the differentiability of the empirical keys among men in various aviation ratings, a random sample of the NVII answer sheets of twenty-five men was drawn from each rating used in the present study and scored on all the thirteen basic keys (AD, BM, CS, CT, DC, EM, ET, FC, GM, HM, QM, RD, and SK) plus the AT key. In addition, two new empirical keys were built for aviation structural mechanics (AM) and aviation ordnancemen (AO) in the hope that they might add further to differentiation among aviation ratings. The new AM and AO keys were built from criterion and cross-validation samples gathered independently of the sample used in this study. Mean profiles were drawn for each of these random samples on all sixteen keys used. On the basis of these profiles twelve empirical keys were chosen that showed promise of differentiating men in a particular aviation rating from those in another. Those retained for use in this study were AD, GM, ET, RD, CT, QM, EM, BM, DC, SK, AT, and AM.

After the answer sheets of all airmen had been scored on the twelve final empirical keys, raw scores were converted to Navy standard scores. This required translating the raw score, X, into a standard score, Z_x, with the standard score distribution having a mean of 50 and a standard deviation of 10.

* The NVII answer sheets were made available for the present study through the cooperation of Dr. G. D. Mayo of the Naval Air Technical Training Command at Memphis, Tennessee. In addition, his staff provided IBM cards for this sample of recruits that contained their BTB scores. These cards together with the NVII answer sheets provided the source for the discriminator variables used in the present investigation.

94

Predicting Achievement and Choice of Specialty

The raw scores on the twelve empirical keys of the interest inventory were converted to Navy standard scores for two reasons. First, some of the keys yielded negative scores and since these are a nuisance for IBM equipment to handle, some linear transformation was necessary to get them into positive form. Second, in preference to merely adding a constant, the alternative of conversion to Navy standard score was chosen since this reduced the scores on all the discriminator variables to the same interpretative base. Although the standardization population for the BTB scores was not used for the interest scores, a standardization population very nearly approaching it was used. It consisted of 400 Navy men in general who were drawn randomly in the same proportion as the various Navy ratings were represented in the total Navy complement as of 1951.

The next step in designing this study was to obtain criterion data. Permission was granted by the chief of Naval personnel to follow up the airmen recruits through their advancement-in-rate listings at the Naval Examining Center at Great Lakes, Illinois. Of the original 1971 members of the sample it was possible to follow up 1544 of them. Of these, 1318 men had advanced in a rating, which provided enough men to permit analysis of results.

The criterion finally chosen was an individual's Navy standard score on the achievement test for his rating the first time he "struck" for third class. Although second-class data were available for some members of the sample, they were very limited. If this had been chosen as the criterion measure, so many members of the original sample would have been without criterion data that it would have been necessary to drop many more ratings from the analysis and, in addition, no cross-validation of results would have been possible.

The final sample of 1318 men was split into a validation group and a cross-validation group as shown in Table 40. It was decided that five of the ratings had too few cases to warrant pulling out a cross-validation sample and that using all the available cases in these five ratings to calculate the discriminant functions for the validation group would be more likely to give stable functions. This was considered more desirable than calculating these functions from a small number of cases and then observing how well they classified men in an equally small cross-validation sample. In each of the remaining six ratings, the cases were randomly drawn into a validation and a cross-validation sample. The size of these groups was chosen so that discriminant functions would be stable and yet as many cases as possible could be used for cross-validation purposes.

The Vocational Interests of Nonprofessional Men

Table 40. Size of Validation and Cross-Validation Groups
in the Final Sample

Rating	Validation	Cross-Validation Group	Total
AB (aviation boatswain's mate)	60	77	137
AC (air controlman)	53		53
AD (aviation machinist's mate)	99	128	227
AE (aviation electrician's mate)	67	90	157
AG (aerographer's mate)	67		67
AK (aviation storekeeper)	42		42
AM (aviation structural mechanic) ...	70	90	160
AO (aviation ordnanceman)	60	72	132
AT (aviation electronics technician)	99	110	209
PH (photographer's mate)	81		81
TD (tradevman)	53		53
Total	751	567	1,318

The essentially taxonomic nature of the present study makes the multiple discriminant analysis model particularly appropriate. As Tatsuoka and Tiedeman (1954) so clearly have pointed out, discriminant analysis can concern itself with any or all of three possible considerations: (1) what are the *distances* that separate any two of the groups under study (differences and similarities between job groups); (2) what are the locations of these groups in a reduced canonical test space (configuration of job families and identification of an occupational hierarchy); and (3) how well can we classify individuals into appropriate groups using their test scores alone (assignment of personnel)? This study considers all three of these issues and thus is concerned with both the problem of testing significance and the problem of estimation.

Discriminant analysis only indicates the group to which an individual is the most similar in terms of the discriminator variables used in the analysis. An evaluation of likelihood of success in that group is not a characteristic of the multiple discriminant technique. On the other hand, this information is exactly that which multiple regression analysis provides. It indicates how likely an individual is of being successful in a particular group, but it cannot assign the individual to the group in which he has the greatest likelihood of being successful. Discriminant analysis aims at maximizing the between-groups variance; regression analysis concentrates on maximizing the within-groups variance. Despite the incompatibility of these two goals, the attractive features of each kind of analysis suggest the desirability of trying to include certain aspects of both in a study of the relation between job choice and measured interests. As a peripheral problem the present study attempted to contrast a routine discriminant analysis with a simple integration of both of the above-mentioned kinds of information in the following way. The entire analysis actually was made on three sets of data. Set I consisted of all the 751 cases distributed across the eleven groups in the validation sample shown in Table 40. This was considered to be the usual discriminant analysis. In addition, within each of the eleven groups members were ordered on the criterion variable. Each group then was split into the top half and the bottom half. Set II data consisted of the top half from each of the eleven groups. Set III data consisted of the bottom half from each of the eleven groups. The purpose was to see whether Set I or Set II discriminant functions would do a better job of classifying people in the upper 50 per cent into their group of membership, and whether Set I or Set III discriminant functions would do a better job of classifying people in the lower 50 per cent into their group of membership. It seemed reasonable to speculate that perhaps discriminant functions based on only "successful" or even on only "unsuccessful" members of the groups might do a better job of correct classification than discriminant functions based on the entire membership in a group. Dividing the criterion groups in half resulted in some small numbers (N's ranged from 21 to 50). This may have led to unstable or unrepresentative functions. The greater heterogeneity in the Set I data, too, may have contributed to greater differentiation among groups and, consequently, to better classification. Tiedeman and Bryan (1954) have discussed the idea that the only information on success that can be attributed to discriminant analysis is that which is introduced into the definition of group membership. The Set II and Set III analyses done as part of this study may provide suggestive evidence on this point.

A cluster analysis based on the pairwise intergroup distances (D²'s) was done for each set of data following the methods suggested by Rao (1950, pp. 361–63). The pair of groups with the smallest intergroup distance was selected as the nucleus of the first cluster. For the remaining groups, those with the smallest distance from each of the members of the cluster were identified. The group with the smallest average distance from the groups already in the cluster was selected as the third member of the cluster. The process of adding groups to the cluster was continued so long as the average distance between the next nearest group and the cluster did not jump

97

markedly, and so long as the members of the cluster were closer to each other than to any other configuration of groups in the space. When the first cluster was determined, the remaining groups were examined. Of these, the pair of groups with the smallest intergroup distance was selected as the nucleus of the second cluster. This procedure was continued until all the groups were exhausted and all the clusters were defined. The computational scheme followed for finding the clusters for Set I, II, and III data is presented in Table 41, 42, and 43.

The same number of clusters with the same group membership emerged in the Set I and Set III data. In the Set II data it was possible to pull out two clusters from what had been a single cluster in the Set I and Set III data. By examining the group membership of the Set II clusters, we could suggest cluster labels. The group membership of the first cluster consists of AD, AM, AE, AB, and AO. This appears to be an aviation maintenance clustering of groups. This same cluster with identical membership emerged in the Set I and Set III data also. The second cluster in the Set II data is composed of AC, AG, and PH, which might be called an aviation operational cluster. The third cluster is composed of AT and TD, an aviation technician cluster. In the Set I and Set III data no separation between the operational groups and the technician groups was apparent, and, consequently, these five groups merged together into one cluster. The fourth cluster in the Set

Table 41. Computational Scheme for Finding Clusters for Set I
(Entire Criterion Membership)

Group Added to Cluster	ΣD^2	No. of D^2's (n)	Increase in ΣD^2/Increase in n	Average D^2 ($\Sigma D^2/n$)
AD-AM	0.540	1	....	0.54
AB	1.963	3	0.712	0.65
AO	5.241	6	1.093	0.87
AE	10.173	10	1.233	1.02
AK	23.216	15	2.609	1.55
CLUSTER I: AD, AM, AB, AO, AE				
AG-PH	0.567	1	....	0.57
AC	2.287	3	0.860	0.76
AT	6.064	6	1.259	1.01
TD	11.956	10	1.473	1.20
AK	29.097	15	3.428	1.94
CLUSTER II: AG, PH, AC, AT, TD				
AK	0.00	1	....	0.00
CLUSTER III: AK				

98

Table 42. Computational Scheme for Finding Clusters for Set II
(Top Half of Criterion Groups)

Group Added to Cluster	ΣD^2	No. of D^2's (n)	Increase in ΣD^2/Increase in n	Average D^2 ($\Sigma D^2/n$)
AD-AM	0.576	1	....	0.58
AE	3.034	3	1.229	1.01
AB	7.906	6	1.624	1.32
AO	13.957	10	1.513	1.40
AK	29.001	15	3.009	1.93
CLUSTER I: AD, AM, AE, AB, AO				
AC-AG	1.063	1	....	1.06
PH	3.706	3	1.322	1.24
AT	9.760	6	2.018	1.63
CLUSTER II: AC, AG, PH				
AT-TD	1.192	1	....	1.19
AK	7.855	3	3.332	2.62
CLUSTER III: AT, TD				
AK	0.00	1	....	0.00
CLUSTER IV: AK				

Table 43. Computational Scheme for Finding Clusters for Set III
(Bottom Half of Criterion Groups)

Group Added to Cluster	ΣD^2	No. of D^2's (n)	Increase in ΣD^2/Increase in n	Average D^2 ($\Sigma D^2/n$)
AO-AB	0.610	1	....	0.61
AD	2.350	3	0.870	0.78
AM	6.516	6	1.389	1.09
AE	14.516	10	2.000	1.45
AK	31.554	15	3.408	2.10
CLUSTER I: AO, AB, AD, AM, AE				
AG-PH	0.659	1	....	0.66
AT	2.374	3	0.858	0.79
AC	6.427	6	1.351	1.07
TD	13.528	10	1.775	1.35
AK	37.675	15	4.829	2.51
CLUSTER II: AG, PH, AT, AC, TD				
AK	0.000	1	....	0.00
CLUSTER III: AK				

The Vocational Interests of Nonprofessional Men

II data had only one group, AK, and this cluster can be described as clerical. This same one-group clerical cluster emerged in the Set I and Set III data also.

Tables 44, 45, and 46 show the average intracluster and intercluster distance (D^2) for all three sets of data. The smallest values in these tables lie on the diagonal, reflecting cluster homogeneity. The nondiagonal values are larger, indicating the greater average distance between groups in different clusters than between groups within a cluster.

For classification purposes discriminant function coefficients and their corresponding correction terms were used to obtain a properly weighted combination of scores on the original variables. Eleven L scores (one for each group) were computed from the Set I data for each individual in the validation sample. In addition, eleven L scores from the Set II data were computed for each individual in the top half of his criterion group, and eleven L scores from the Set III data were computed for each individual in the bottom half of his criterion group. L scores for all three sets of data were computed for each individual in the cross-validation sample. These sets of eleven L scores then were examined and each individual was as-

Table 44. Average Intracluster and Intercluster D^2 for Set I
(Entire Criterion Membership)

Cluster	I	II	III
I (AD, AM, AB, AO, AE).........	1.02	3.26	2.61
II (AG, PH, AC, AT, TD)..........	3.26	1.20	3.43
III (AK)	2.61	3.43	0.00

Table 45. Average Intracluster and Intercluster D^2 for Set II
(Top Half of Criterion Groups)

Cluster	I	II	III	IV
I (AD, AM, AE, AB, AO)..	1.40	4.25	4.26	3.01
II (AC, AG, PH)..........	4.25	1.24	2.14	2.71
III (AT, TD)..............	4.26	2.14	1.19	3.93
IV (AK)	3.01	2.71	3.93	0.00

Table 46. Average Intracluster and Intercluster D^2 for Set III
(Bottom Half of Criterion Groups)

Cluster	I	II	III
I (AO, AB, AD, AM, AE)	1.45	3.77	3.41
II (AG, PH, AT, AC, TD)	3.77	1.35	4.83
III (AK)	3.41	4.83	0.00

Table 47. Classification of Individuals in the Top Half of Criterion Groups in the Validation Sample into Groups by Highest L Scores on Set I and Set II Discriminant Functions

Observed Group Membership	No.	Group into Which Classified										
		AB	AC	AD	AE	AG	AK	AM	AO	AT	PH	TD
Set I Discriminant Functions												
AB	30	*3*[a]	0	6	3	4	6	3	3	1	1	0
AC	26	1	*12*	0	2	0	3	1	0	2	2	3
AD	50	5	2	*14*	6	0	2	12	1	3	0	5
AE	33	2	2	5	*9*	1	4	0	2	8	1	4
AG	34	1	5	1	0	*10*	3	0	1	3	3	2
AK	21	1	1	1	2	1	*7*	0	3	3	1	1
AM	35	3	0	8	3	1	2	*12*	3	1	1	2
AO	30	2	2	4	4	3	3	3	*7*	0	1	1
AT	49	1	4	1	1	5	3	1	0	*16*	1	12
PH	41	0	8	0	2	8	3	3	2	2	*5*	3
TD	26	1	3	2	0	2	2	2	0	4	1	*9*
Set II Discriminant Functions												
AB	30	*11*	0	6	2	2	3	1	4	1	0	0
AC	26	1	*10*	0	3	1	3	1	0	1	3	3
AD	50	6	1	*15*	5	0	0	13	4	4	0	2
AE	33	6	2	5	*11*	2	1	1	2	2	0	1
AG	34	0	5	1	3	*12*	4	0	1	3	2	3
AK	21	1	1	2	0	1	*6*	2	2	2	3	1
AM	35	5	0	5	2	0	2	*14*	5	1	0	1
AO	30	2	0	2	2	2	4	5	*12*	0	1	0
AT	49	1	2	1	2	1	3	1	2	*23*	2	11
PH	41	0	4	1	4	7	3	2	3	2	*12*	3
TD	26	2	2	0	2	2	1	3	1	5	1	*7*

[a] The "correct" classification is indicated by italics.

101

Table 48. Classification of Individuals in the Bottom Half of Criterion Groups in the Validation Sample into Groups by Highest L Scores on Set I and Set III Discriminant Functions

Observed Group Membership	No.	Group into Which Classified										
		AB	AC	AD	AE	AG	AK	AM	AO	AT	PH	TD
Set I Discriminant Functions												
AB	30	8ᵃ	1	1	3	0	4	5	5	2	1	0
AC	27	2	5	0	1	8	2	0	4	2	1	2
AD	49	10	1	*12*	5	0	3	8	5	0	2	3
AE	34	4	3	4	*10*	0	1	3	3	4	1	1
AG	33	4	2	2	3	5	1	1	3	4	5	3
AK	21	3	0	1	2	0	9	2	3	0	0	1
AM	35	7	0	5	4	0	1	*16*	2	1	1	0
AO	30	6	1	2	3	2	4	3	7	1	1	0
AT	50	3	4	0	7	2	3	1	2	*16*	3	9
PH	40	4	0	1	3	9	3	2	2	2	7	7
TD	27	4	0	1	2	0	5	1	0	5	2	7
Set III Discriminant Functions												
AB	30	6	1	3	2	1	2	7	4	3	1	0
AC	27	1	*11*	0	2	4	1	1	2	0	1	4
AD	49	6	3	*14*	5	0	3	8	6	1	1	2
AE	34	1	2	3	*14*	1	1	2	4	3	0	3
AG	33	1	4	2	2	*12*	1	1	1	4	4	1
AK	21	2	2	0	2	0	*10*	2	1	0	0	2
AM	35	4	0	5	5	1	2	*15*	2	0	0	1
AO	30	3	1	4	5	1	3	4	5	0	3	1
AT	50	1	7	0	4	1	3	1	3	*16*	7	7
PH	40	4	5	1	1	5	4	1	0	7	8	4
TD	27	2	2	1	0	1	4	0	0	3	4	*10*

ᵃ The "correct" classification is indicated by italics.

Table 49. Classification of Individuals in the Cross-Validation Sample into Groups by Highest L Scores on Set I, Set II and Set III Discriminant Functions

Observed Group Membership	No.	AB	AC	AD	AE	AG	AK	AM	AO	AT	PH	TD
Set I Discriminant Functions												
AB	77	*14*[a]	2	13	6	0	10	13	13	2	3	1
AD	128	14	3	*22*	15	3	14	32	10	5	1	9
AE	90	17	1	6	*19*	6	7	10	4	10	3	7
AM	90	15	1	15	10	5	2	*20*	11	3	3	5
AO	72	4	10	7	7	1	12	16	*5*	5	4	1
AT	110	6	8	4	12	13	3	6	2	*24*	5	27
Set II Discriminant Functions												
AB	77	*15*	1	14	9	0	8	12	13	3	2	0
AD	128	24	2	*25*	11	1	11	27	19	6	1	1
AE	90	17	1	11	*13*	2	7	9	7	10	7	6
AM	90	24	1	14	2	1	3	*22*	16	2	2	3
AO	72	8	6	9	8	0	11	10	*12*	4	3	1
AT	110	9	6	8	12	6	3	4	7	*34*	9	12
Set III Discriminant Functions												
AB	77	*10*	5	12	7	0	10	16	6	4	3	4
AD	128	13	6	*16*	22	2	19	23	2	12	5	8
AE	90	9	5	5	*10*	9	5	8	4	17	4	14
AM	90	14	4	18	8	5	2	*21*	1	8	4	5
AO	72	6	10	8	7	2	10	12	*2*	4	6	5
AT	110	2	13	1	10	11	2	1	1	*32*	9	28

[a] The "correct" classification is indicated by italics.

103

The Vocational Interests of Nonprofessional Men

signed to the group for which he received the highest L score. The criterion
on which this assignment is based is a maximum likelihood estimate and reduces to a minimum the probability of misclassification. The resulting classifications are shown in Tables 47, 48, and 49.

An individual was considered to be "correctly" classified when he was
assigned to that group of which he was a member. However, this assumption should be viewed with an awareness of possible inherent contradic-
tions. The fact that an individual has achieved some success in a particular
Navy rating does not mean necessarily that he might not have done better
or been more satisfied in another rating. On the other hand, some men may
have raw score profiles that are very different from the mean profile of their
group and yet may be well satisfied with their jobs and highly successful in
them, perhaps by virtue of their being "atypical." Despite the fact that all
"incorrect" classifications may not be real misclassifications and all "correct" classifications may not be correct in the real sense, actual group membership was used as one criterion of correct classification.

A more global view of correctness of classification might be to consider
an individual to be correctly classified when he was assigned to that *cluster*
of which he was a member. Such a criterion seems highly justified in view
of the fact that there was such homogeneity of group profiles within clusters. In many instances, an individual's L score for his group of membership missed being the highest only by the third or fourth decimal place. In
many of these cases, he actually was assigned to a member group in his

Table 50. Classification of Individuals in the Top Half of Criterion
Groups in the Validation Sample into Clusters by Highest L
Scores on Set I and Set II Discriminant Functions

Observed Cluster Membership	No.	Cluster into Which Classified			
		I	II	III	IV
Set I Discriminant Functions					
I	178	*122*[a]	19	20	17
II	101	14	*58*	20	9
III	75	9	20	*41*	5
IV	21	7	3	4	*7*
Set II Discriminant Functions					
I	178	*146*	10	12	10
II	101	20	*56*	15	10
III	75	15	10	*46*	4
IV	21	7	5	3	*6*

[a] The "correct" classification is indicated by italics.

104

Predicting Achievement and Choice of Specialty

cluster, although not to his own group. In view of this, a second analysis of classifications was done by cluster of membership. These results are presented in Tables 50, 51, and 52.

Most of the tests of proportion of correct classification into group of membership in the validation sample were significant beyond the .001 level. However, there was considerable shrinkage in these significance levels when the discriminant functions were applied to the cross-validation sample. AT was the only group that held up well on cross-validation, L scores for all three sets of data showing very little shrinkage.

Table 51. Classification of Individuals in the Bottom Half of Criterion Groups in the Validation Sample into Clusters by Highest L Scores on Set I and Set III Discriminant Functions

Observed Cluster Membership	No.	Cluster into Which Classified		
		I	II	III
Set I Discriminant Functions				
I	178	*141*[a]	24	13
II	177	53	*110*	14
III	21	11	1	*9*
Set III Discriminant Functions				
I	178	*137*	30	11
II	177	32	*132*	13
III	21	7	4	*10*

[a] The "correct" classification is indicated by italics.

Table 52. Classification of Individuals in the Cross-Validation Sample into Clusters by Highest L Scores on Set I, Set II, and Set III Discriminant Functions

Observed Cluster Membership	No.	Cluster into Which Classified			
		I	II	III	IV
Set I Discriminant Functions					
I	457	*318*[a]	94	45	
II	110	30	*77*	3	
Set II Discriminant Functions					
I	457	*351*	30	36	40
III	110	40	21	*46*	3
Set III Discriminant Functions					
I	457	*260*	151	46	
II	110	15	*93*	2	

[a] The "correct" classification is indicated by italics.

The Vocational Interests of Nonprofessional Men

All the tests of proportion of correct classification into *cluster* of membership in the validation sample were significant beyond the .001 level. This same goodness of classification held up in the cross-validation sample too. Although there was some shrinkage, all the tests were significant beyond the .001 level.

It is not completely satisfying from the empirical point of view to be able to say that better than chance classification has been achieved since any classification process must exceed this level of success before it can be described as having any merit. What is really the main concern is how much above the level of chance a particular classification process can attain. The high significance levels found in the present study indicate that a substantial improvement over chance actually was achieved. In order to determine just how great this improvement was, the following ratio was computed:

$$\text{Percentage of improvement} = \frac{o - e}{N - e} \times 100$$

where o is the number correctly classified, e is the number expected to be correctly classified by chance, and N is the total frequency; thus (o − e) is the observed gain over the chance level and (N − e) is the total gain to perfect classification. These percentages are reported in Tables 53 and 54 for classification into *group* and *cluster* of membership for both validation and cross-validation samples. Again the superiority on cross-validation of the AT discriminant functions for classifying AT's into their group of membership was demonstrated. The improvement over the level of chance is even more striking when we examine classification into cluster of membership. Substantial gains over the chance level are apparent in the validation sample, and even on cross-validation the gains are still marked.

The 73 per cent gain over chance in classifying cross-validation AT's into their cluster of membership on the Set III discriminant functions should be examined closely. This high percentage indicates that discriminant functions based on low-achieving individuals assign more AT's in the cross-validation sample into their cluster of membership than the Set I or Set II discriminant functions. This means that Set III functions indiscriminantly pick up most of the AT's, whether high or low achievers, and assign them to Cluster II composed of AG, PH, AT, AC, and TD ratings. In view of the high attrition rate in the Class "A" school for AT's, what is needed is a classification equation that discriminates the potentially high-achieving AT's and sorts them out from the rest of their cluster. The Set II discriminant functions, which were based on high achievers, does a better job of

Table 53. Percentage of Improvement over Chance of Classification into Group of Membership When the Highest L Score Is Used

| | Validation Sample | | | | Cross-Validation Sample | | |
| | Set II | | Set III | | | | |
Group	Set I L Scores	Set II L Scores	Set I L Scores	Set III L Scores	Set I L Scores	Set II L Scores	Set III L Scores
AB	4.93	30.15	14.10	12.82	6.65	2.87	3.83
AC	39.91	33.69	14.66	34.07			
AD	18.92	22.10	18.18	21.70	6.09	6.12	2.15
AE	20.48	26.25	20.29	33.77	10.18	5.25	−0.20
AG	22.15	29.67	8.85	31.44			
AK	25.81	22.36	36.81	42.41			
AM	27.10	32.24	38.89	35.67	6.17	11.31	10.55
AO	18.79	33.63	15.22	9.97	−1.07	4.15	−0.04
AT	23.93	39.88	24.80	24.58	14.42	22.88	17.95
PH	18.76	14.44	12.12	13.30			
TD	26.38	20.10	18.80	30.58			

Table 54. Percentage of Improvement over Chance of Classification into Cluster of Membership When the Highest L Score Is Used

| | Validation Sample | | | | Cross-Validation Sample | | |
| | Set II | | Set III | | | | |
Cluster	Set I L Scores	Set II L Scores	Set I L Scores	Set III L Scores	Set I L Scores	Set II L Scores	Set III L Scores
I	47.09	63.95	54.29	56.70	21.25	25.28	16.29
II	41.95	43.17	40.94	54.48	57.05		72.87
III	41.38	51.51	36.81	42.41		31.98	
IV	25.81	22.36					

making this kind of discriminating selection. If, however, assignment to cluster of membership is the desired goal, then the Set III discriminant functions do the best job for AT's.

From these results it can be concluded that there is a definite advantage to be gained by taking into account information on success in the definition of criterion membership. On the whole, the Set II discriminant functions, which were based on individuals in the top half of their criterion groups, showed a significant superiority over both Set I and Set III functions for classifying individuals into both group and cluster of membership. This superiority was demonstrated conclusively in the cross-validation sample.

The final stage of the analysis involved a canonical reduction of the original raw score variables to determine the minimum number of independent dimensions necessary to account for most of the variability among groups

The Vocational Interests of Nonprofessional Men

Table 55. Proportion of Total Variance Accounted for by Each Canonical Variable

Canonical Variable	Set I	Set II	Set III
1	.5947	.5618	.5708
2	.0000	.0000	.0000
3	.1510	.1618	.1140
4	.0000	.0000	.0000
5	.0113	.0595	.0355
6	.0000	.0000	.0000
7	.0000	.0000	.0410
8	.0000	.0000	.0000
9	.0000	.0757	.0665
10	.0927	.0243	.1292
11	.0032	.0557	.0000
12	.0321	.0049	.0038
13	.0542	.0190	.0000
14	.0099	.0077	.0209
15	.0202	.0000	.0083
16	.0306	.0295	.0100

on the discriminator variables. Table 55 indicates the proportion of total variance accounted for by each of the sixteen canonical roots. Most notable of the characteristics of this table is the large number of zero or negligible weights; in each of our three sets of data 90 per cent of the variance in the test battery that produces group differences can be accounted for by five variables. Since the two largest roots accounted for two-thirds to three-fourths of the among-groups variability for the three sets of data, two-dimensional geometric representations of the locations of the job group centroids in this reduced test space were prepared. The clustering of groups that emerged from the preliminary cluster analysis of the intergroup distances (D^2's) was strikingly demonstrated by this procedure, corroborating the picture of job family organization for all three sets of data.

The nature of such canonical variables is not necessarily such as to make them the most desirable measures of interests and abilities. Canonical variables do not represent unitary dimensions in the psychological sense. Canonical reduction has the same disadvantages in interpretation as a principal component factor analysis where no rotation to "psychological meaningfulness" is attempted. Nevertheless, it should be profitable to examine the compositions of the most significant canonical variables for insights into the role that ability and interest measures play in job group discrimination. Table 56 presents the weights assigned to the original variables in

Table 56. Weights Assigned to Each Original Variable in Order to Produce Canonical Variables Z_1 and Z_3

Original Variable	Entire Criterion Membership	Top Half of Criterion	Bottom Half of Criterion
First Canonical Variable (Z_1)			
With positive weights			
GCT	.060	.069	.065
ARI	.037	.025	.052
MAT	.011	.012	.027
CLER	.010	.020	
ET	.017		.039
QM	.012		.032
RD		.013	
EM		.010	.023
SK		.012	
AT		.048	
DC			.015
With negative weights			
AD	.025	.018	.029
GM	.017	.042	
BM	.034	.015	.044
SK	.021		.034
CT		.013	
AT			.036
Third Canonical Variable (Z_3)			
With positive weights			
ARI	.021	.030	
MAT	.032	.035	
RD	.014		.063
CT	.045	.043	
EM	.028	.029	
DC	.017	.029	
AT	.012		.096
BM			.011
AD		.040	
GM		.011	
ET		.035	
With negative weights			
GCT	.010		
CLER	.043	.043	.017
ET	.012		.062
QM	.066	.031	.059
BM	.013	.022	
SK	.047	.028	.117
MAT			.012
CT			.042
EM			.067
AM		.032	.046
AT		.027	

order to generate each of the two most powerful canonical variables. These weights suggest the nature of the canonical variable.

It appears that Z_1 is a positive function of general intellectual ability in the highly technical electronic and numerical areas and a function of negative interests in low-level mechanical activities. This variable one is tempted to describe simply as "g." This is probably not sufficient, for there are evidences of an occupational hierarchy factor, perhaps a "desire to do something hard" component.

Canonical variable Z_3 is much more difficult to interpret. Positive contributions come from the arithmetical variable which is orthogonal to the arithmetical variable of Z_1. Perhaps this means that whereas the Z_1 arithmetical loading was for a number factor, a different sort of factor is represented here, one that deals with the electrical-mechanical complex of electricity, communication systems, etc. The role of electronics in this canonical variable is somewhat ambiguous since interest in electronics contributes very heavily to Z_3 for the bottom half of the criterion group and very negatively for the top half of the criterion group. It appears that the character of Z_3 is quite different for low achievers. The weight given to AT on both Z_1 and Z_3 is the most outstanding feature that discriminates low achievers from high achievers. Experience in naval air technical training has testified to this fact through the inordinately high attrition rate in the Class "A" school for AT's.

It is clear how we should interpret Z_3 with respect to what it is inversely related to. There are heavy negative loadings on interest in clerical activities, probably of the routine, desk-bound variety. The value of canonical reduction is not diminished by the difficulty in making a psychological interpretation of the canonical variables. The ability to characterize in a quantitative fashion a job group's location in reduced canonical test space can add substantially to the identification of job group communalities and can increase our understanding of the psychological organization of the occupational domain we are investigating.

The preceding analysis may call to mind for the technical reader the work of Thorndike and Hagen (1959). There are certain similarities between their study and ours. Ours was a follow-up into Navy careers of naval airmen technicians tested as recruits; theirs was a follow-up into civilian occupations of Air Force cadets tested during World War II. Both studies were concerned with the degree to which it is possible to classify men into their later occupational areas on the basis of an optimal combination of their test scores.

The similarity in design of these two studies makes certain comparisons possible. Most readers will agree that the results of the Thorndike and Hagen study were very disappointing. They achieved little success with their data in accomplishing either of two possible objectives, i.e., (1) maximizing within-groups variance to permit effective prediction of success within occupations, and (2) maximizing among-groups variance to permit discriminating between job groups. A comparison of the canonical reductions done in the two studies is especially interesting. The canonical reduction performed on the Thorndike and Hagen data yielded very little separation between job groups despite the fact that they had selected a rather widely dispersed set of occupations to analyze. In our study the job groups were far more homogeneous in nature, all technical ground support to naval aviation; this would appear to make job group discrimination a much more difficult task, yet the observed separation between groups is strikingly clear in the naval aviation study. Thorndike and Hagen suggest that their failure to achieve good discrimination between groups may be attributed to the highly selected nature of the sample population with which they were working (all men were screened on a test for admission to aviation cadet training and by their own choice to apply). However, our sample population was subject to this same kind of selection (all men were screened on the Navy Basic Test Battery for admission to naval air technical training and by their own choice to apply).

Some estimate of the degree to which the two studies accomplished their objectives may be obtained by examining an index of discrimination reported in the Thorndike and Hagen study (1959, p. 316). They report having obtained a ratio of among-groups variance to within-groups variance of 0.471. The same ratios for Sets I, II, and III of Albitz's data are 1.107, 1.446, and 1.355, respectively. Such markedly larger values reflect the greater discrimination among groups which was achieved in the Albitz study. The index of separation among groups in the top half of our criterion groups (Set II) is three times as large as that obtained by Thorndike and Hagen. What produces this great difference in results?

It is evident that Thorndike and Hagen assumed that classification of workers into a great variety of occupations could be accomplished with some success by means of the limited battery of test scores available to them. It is true that they point out the possible limitations in the scope of the test battery they were using but they offer this as one of several suggested explanations for the paucity of good results rather than recognizing it as a critical deficiency in the design of their study. If we look for a moment at the realm of aptitude tests alone, their aptitude battery did not even contain a clerical test. A far more serious deficiency was the lack of any measures of vocational interests, not to mention other areas such as attitudes, personality characteristics, motivation. There are many sources of information which would suggest that correct occupational classification is better achieved when measured interests are used rather than aptitudes. Considerable evidence for this point of view has been mentioned in earlier pages of this volume.

Thus, it is very instructive to have the analysis of the Air Force data at hand at a time when an evaluation of our data is being made, for it makes very impressive the point that interest measures are of primary importance in occupational choice and in the prediction of occupational group membership. The earlier report of the work by Norman (1957) which was presented in Chapter 5 also has a bearing here, for that study used only interest measures in determining the differentiation between 115 fairly diverse occupational groups. With no aptitude measures in his test battery, but with occupational groups of approximately the same diversity as those selected for the Thorndike and Hagen discriminant analysis, Norman obtained a ratio of among-groups variance to within-groups variance of 1.857. The degree of separation between groups in Norman's dispersion analysis is almost four times as great as that obtained by Thorndike and Hagen and he employed very similar kinds of job groups. One cannot escape the obvious conclusion that when the problem is one of prediction of occupational choice or occupational classification, the use of interest measures should receive more consideration than the use of aptitude measures.

✦ 7 ✦

Toward an Improved Set of Interest Measures

A THOUGHTFUL review of the great amount of research in the domain of interest measurement surely is appropriate and long overdue. Much of the current activity aims to develop another Strong VIB, or to make a new and better Kuder Preference Record, or to demonstrate that the best type of item to use is one that is pictorial, is related to specific tasks, or is forced-choice in form. Or else emphasis is placed on ease of scoring, or on factorial content, or on the simplicity of the display when scores are presented.

The work reported in the preceding chapters suggests that there can be somewhat more orderliness in interest measurement than has yet been observed, and that such orderliness will emerge if appropriate developmental procedures are followed. The data do not quite demonstrate this, but certainly do suggest that this is the direction which succeeding work should take. For if our current findings are supported by the work of others, we should be able to develop measures of vocational interests which (1) have orderly and meaningful structure within themselves, (2) have substantial predictive power in identifying occupations in which a person is likely to remain, and, presumably, to be contented, (3) have predictive value in educational and training settings, and (4) have meaningful relationships to other measures of the individual personality. Besides this, such measures would be developed in terms of individuals, not jobs, and so would involve a small rather than a very large number of dimensions.

Let us review some of these matters in greater detail, in order that the general philosophy developed during the course of the program of research reported here may be fully revealed — either to be attacked if incorrect, or to be a source of guidance in other research if meritorious.

Vocational interest measures have ordinarily represented a separate family of measures when used by counselors. They are classified neither as personality measures nor as aptitude measures. They are usually put into the special category of "interests," are treated as though they have no orderly relationship to other measures, and ordinarily are used in an entirely different way from these other measures of individual characteristics. In a sense, they do not belong in the usual test battery, but force their way into such a battery because they have been shown to be highly effective in separating employed workers in various occupations.

Obviously, the nature of individual vocational preferences should not require the development of a new scale for every vocational opportunity. Therefore it follows, as I believe most persons would agree, that there should be fewer scoring keys for an interest inventory than there are occupations even if we are interested in counseling students about their opportunities for growth and advancement in any one of many occupations. But if we reduce from a very large number to, say, forty, have we changed our point of view? Do we *need* forty scoring keys?

This problem I would like to refer to as the problem of choice between an open scoring system and a closed scoring system. The open system is oriented toward the world of work and aims to reflect each major occupation in that world of work. When a new occupation develops, someone must determine whether or not a new scoring key is required. The closed system is oriented toward the individual, and aims to reflect each of the major dimensions of interest on which individuals differ. Unless some new evidence appeared to show that the latter scoring system failed to assess a dimension, there would not arise an occasion when a new scale would be added.

The Strong Vocational Interest Blank is an ideal instrument to illustrate the open system of scoring. Keys now have been developed for many of the major occupations which college students enter; new keys have been in process of development continuously since the blank was published. The Kuder Preference Record, Vocational, is an obvious illustration of the closed system. With the exception of the addition of the outdoors key, the preference record has remained unchanged in number of scores since its inception.

Can vocational interest measures developed by examining the character-

istics of individuals be functionally equivalent to measures obtained by examining the characteristics of jobs? Will such measures have orderly and
sensible and understandable relationships both to other measures of the
individual (personality, values, and aptitudes) and to later occupational
choice? I believe the answer to each of these questions is yes. Measures of
motivation should relate to personality dimensions and to the personal values which a person holds. Measured interests should have low but greater
than zero correlations with certain aptitude measures. What results would
be obtained if we studied the *appropriate* dimensions of interests as these
relate to other personal characteristics?

This question has import for the better understanding of the development and maturing of vocational interests. We usually find that bright
youngsters are interested in natural science. For some persons these interests persist; for others, interests grow in social problems and matters of
human welfare. Many counselors comment on the expected increase in interests in social service areas with age. If we employed better measures of
vocational interest, would not our observations of such phenomena be
more accurate, and our understanding greater?

Furthermore, what is it in the background of some individuals that leads
them to be likely to succeed in *any* endeavor they begin? Our measures of
interests have primarily attended to differences between occupations. I believe it is time that we look at the possibilities of measuring some sort of
generalized motivation which relates to degree of occupational success. It
is true that in the preceding chapters some work on this has been reported,
but this work has been minor and relatively insignificant in comparison to
the magnitude of the problem. It is clear that our society today makes great
demands on some persons and obtains from certain of these persons responses which are equally great, but there are others on whom no great demands are made and who yet do achieve a great deal. How do we make
predictions of the differential strength of ambition or the magnitude of
drive?

Also omitted from the preceding chapters because of the way in which
the work is reported, and because of the orientation of our investigations,
is any study of individual differences in breadth of interest. Yet we know
that some persons evidence great interest in many more areas than do others. On the Kuder Preference Record it is impossible to reflect this because
a person cannot make very high scores on all scales. On the Strong Vocational Interest Blank this is unlikely to emerge in the way we would like to

The Vocational Interests of Nonprofessional Men

see it because the scales tend to be contaminated by differences in the breadth of interest within various occupational groups. Certainly it ought to be possible to get a measure of the characteristic we might call versatility or flexibility. Some individuals surely would be equally content in any one of 20 or 30 or 40 or 50 occupations whereas others are going to be fairly discontent in most and only modestly happy in the one occupation which suits them best.

Along this same line in the measurement of interest, it would be very useful to have some devices that would reflect the style of the individual. The work of Stogdill and Koehler (1952) has shown that executives behave differently. Some executives play primarily a public relations role; others are essentially production managers; others are essentially fiscal agents. This difference among workers in a single field is evident at the skilled trades level as well. Among electricians in a union local, for example, there will be some persons with very high scores on the electrician key who are quite inactive in union affairs, whereas there are other electricians scoring fairly low on that key who are the union leaders and organizers, or who participate in all sorts of community affairs. This style of work may occasionally indicate a rejection of the primary occupational membership. But in some instances this is not the case. Rather, it indicates a selection of those tasks or functions within the occupation that are the most challenging to the individual. We have seen in the development of specialty keys for psychologists, for example, an effective use of additional scoring procedures for breaking a profession into a number of sub-parts. The same sort of thing has been done with medical and engineering specialties. However, there are additional variables which might also be attacked.

It is also obvious that there are distinct relationships between interests and the choice of school subjects. Most of the investigations which have been done heretofore have shown little such relationship. Yet the data collected in the course of the work I have done suggest that when school subjects are broken into meaningful categories there are substantial differences between the mean scores on various interest keys of students in these various areas of specialization. An excellent place to find such differences is among students in various specialties in an industrial high school or institute. However, I think it ought to be easily observed that differences exist among students in medical schools, students in colleges of education, students in law schools, and the like. These differences not only exist, they also are useful in predicting relative success in school subjects of persons of equal aptitude. Yet the aptitude variables carry such a substantial amount of the predictable variance that we frequently overlook the role of the interest measures in this regard.

It is important to note in some of the materials reviewed in preceding chapters that a combination of interests and aptitudes is superior to the use of either interests or aptitudes alone. This is the case not only when we are attempting to predict success in school subjects but also when we are trying to classify workers into various fields. It should be noted in passing that the nature of the aptitude battery and of the interest battery surely must vary depending on the level of jobs that we are talking about but that even when we are working with only a small range of the aptitude variables the contribution of the combined scores is substantial both for classification and for prediction. The work of Albitz suggests that this classification process will occur best when we are looking primarily at the more able members of occupational groups.

These various notions about what can be expected from improved methods of interest measurement place a certain burden on me to summarize in rather explicit form the way in which this improvement is to be accomplished. The reader should recognize that these stipulations are made on the basis of current understanding, and not on the basis of observations which come as these steps are employed. Even so, any investigator should be willing to make some estimates about steps most likely to prove fruitful.

The first step in such a review is to suggest the most beneficial way in which our "best" interest measures would be used by a counselor. Interest measures should provide data on the *direction* for an individual to take, as against *level*. Aptitude measures indicate something about the general level of the occupation; at any one level there are a wide variety of occupations each requiring substantially different interest patterns for the employee. The direction in which the individual should move is suggested much more by interest measures than by aptitude variables.

Obviously our counselor wants to move beyond the stereotype, that is, to know not merely whether a person thinks it would be great to be called a physician but also whether he would enjoy the activities which a physician must engage in and whether he would find sufficient motivation to complete medical training. What the counselor needs to know is the way in which the individual differs from his peer group and how these differences relate to his probable final vocational objective. The *difference from his peer group* is the critical part, for we would expect that at a particular age most youngsters express interest in becoming aviators or in becoming physicians or in becoming electronics technicians or explorers, or some such. Paying attention to the way in which persons differ from each other at a given age level permits us to avoid being trapped by the trends which occur from age to age.

With these points in mind, let us then review the principles which will possibly lead us to develop the type of interest measure that will be most useful to the counselor. First, we assume that there are differences among persons at a given level of education or at a given age in their responses to an interest inventory. We also assume that these differences in responses are related to differences in their preferences for activities at that particular time. We assume that these responses have validity, although not necessarily in terms of some sort of eternal, permanent, unchanging response patterns; rather we assume that the responses made at a given point in time have some predictive value in suggesting the later decisions that a person will make in selecting occupational fields. We also assume then that changes which occur in interests from age to age are predicable; that is, that these changes occur over all age groups, and that the differences *between individuals* remain relatively constant. This means that any keys which capitalize upon the differences between persons at one age level will be predictive of differences between these persons at a later age. The scores that we use therefore become stable over time. This is a critical point (and not yet fully supported by data) in the development of interest measures.

This set of principles suggests that we should examine employed workers to determine what differences exist between occupational groups in their measured interests. We should look at the differences in their responses to individual items of an inventory. If we select our group well, and have developed a good inventory, we will find a large number of responses which yield very large differences between groups — differences so large that we need not use any item responses of doubtful statistical significance. We will use these differences to develop scoring keys and will then score such employed workers and other employed groups on the key we have developed. We will attempt to get additional criterion groups to make sure that the observed differences are stable and can be generalized from one sample of workers in an occupation to another sample.

At the same time that this is done we will need to investigate the way in which interest responses cluster, using samples of persons of some given age. We might use, for example, employed workers in a variety of occupations or we might use a sample of high school seniors. But our intent would be to find the clusters of responses which provide relatively homogeneous scales. These homogeneous scales then could be used to score responses of inventories of employed workers, inventories of high school groups, and the like. These procedures should yield two sets of scores, one set having an orderly relationship to the other. Thus the world of work ought to reflect the same dimensions of interest that you can find by examining individuals without reference to the work they are doing. We have found this so in our work. Other investigators would, I think, also find this to be the case if they analyzed inventory responses without permitting their own preconceptions about people or about the world of work to influence the judgments they make in the analysis of data. This may be hard to do: hardly any investigators whose work I have studied have been able completely to divorce themselves from such preconceptions in their analysis of data. E. K. Strong has come closest.

These steps must provide us with a measure which can be used in a counseling setting. Which of the two types of scores should we use? Perhaps neither. I think it likely that the best measure would be a combination of the empirical key which is developed by looking at the world of work and the homogeneous key which is developed by looking at individuals. We would use a combination in order to capitalize upon the advantages gained by two different ways of looking at the same variable.

A combination of scores derived from two such different procedures seems odd and improper. Perhaps it is also unwise. But the empirical scores are superior to homogeneous scores in separating employed occupational groups, while the homogeneous keys have integrity, have desired psychometric characteristics, and are few in number. And the two types of keys for the same area have correlations almost as high as their reliabilities. Why not use the desired dimensionality of the homogeneous keys in combination with the proven validity of the empirical key? I would suggest this be done by adding to the homogeneous key a moderate number of highly valid items which have at least some correlation with the homogeneous key. This would provide a small number of highly efficient scoring keys.

This set of scores could be used with persons at the high school level, at the trades school level, at the college level, and in the field of employment. When we use such scores with high school students, we will need to show the degree to which an individual differs from his peers in high school on scores on various keys. In other words, a high school student's scores should not be compared with those of an employed worker. Rather he should be compared with other high school students. When we deal with college students, the scores ought to indicate the way in which the individual differs from other college students. When we work with employed persons we should compare their scores with other employed workers. At the same time that we do this, however, we ought to show where the employed workers fall as a standard reference point, in order to show where the criterion group falls on each one of these keys.

Almost every counselor would like to be able to think about the world of work in some sort of orderly fashion. I believe it is possible to do this by the use of measured interests. What we can do is to establish families of occupations by relating the scores of persons employed in one occupational group to the scores of workers in other occupational groups on each of the interest dimensions with which we are working. I would propose, for example, that we define (and name) a key on an interest inventory in terms of the hierarchy of occupational group mean scores on that key. Thus a key which yields a very high mean score when taken by electricians and which yields a very low mean score when taken by salesmen might be called an electrician key or a negative sales key. The name given to the key must be chosen carefully, since counselors have a tendency to reify these variables and to read into the title much more than ought to be there. Perhaps a key should be defined in innocuous terms such as are sometimes used with personality measures; then the meaning of the keys will be generated by the observed scores of various occupational groups. This provides an opportunity for a counselor to learn about occupations in the very process of using the interest inventory.

The counselor also can be informed about the way in which occupations cluster in n-dimensional space when all interest scores are used at once. The preceding chapter has shown the way in which this can be done and I trust has impressed the reader with the value of this approach to occupational classification.

It is unfortunate that the huge amount of work which has been done in the measurement of vocational interest has yielded so little information about the way in which these interests develop and the way in which these interests relate to other aspects of the individual. It is also unfortunate that this vast amount of work has given us so little insight into the nature of the world of work. I believe that the procedures which have been outlined in the preceding paragraphs for the development of an interest inventory will yield a device which will have great value not only for the counseling of individuals but also for the understanding of the processes by which occupational choice occur. This, it seems to me, ought to be the ultimate goal of work in vocational interest measurement.

This review suggests that the Minnesota Vocational Interest Inventory has usefulness at this time for counseling and research purposes. The inventory would be improved by some reduction in length and by somewhat simpler scoring. These steps are planned. But it will serve its greatest function if it is used widely enough to permit the collection of substantial amounts of data. I hope the point of this research has become clear to the reader — that the use of a vocational interest inventory provides not only an aid to counselors, but a basis for better understanding of the world of occupations, and of the processes of decision which individuals go through as they make an occupational choice.

REFERENCES AND INDEX

References

Albitz, Diane R. *A discriminant analysis of the aptitudes and interests of enlisted men in eleven naval aviation groups.* Minneapolis: University of Minnesota, Department of Psychology, Technical Report No. 9, 1958.

Clemans, W. V. *An analytical and empirical examination of some properties of ipsative measures.* Seattle: University of Washington, 1956.

Cronbach, L. J. Coefficient alpha and the internal structure of tests. *Psychometrika,* 1951, 16, 297–334.

Darley, J. G., and Theda Hagenah. *Vocational interest measurement.* Minneapolis: University of Minnesota Press, 1955.

DuBois, P., Jane Loevinger, and Goldine Gleser. *The construction of homogeneous keys for a biographical inventory.* San Antonio, Texas: Human Resources Research Center, Lackland Air Force Base Research Bulletin, 52-18, 1952.

Edwards, A. L. *Edwards Personal Preference Schedule.* New York: Psychological Corporation, 1954, 1959.

Gee, Helen H. A comparison of empirical and homogeneous keys in interest measurement. Unpublished doctoral dissertation, University of Minnesota, 1955.

———, and K. E. Clark. *A comparison of empirical and homogeneous keys in interest measurement.* Minneapolis: University of Minnesota, Department of Psychology, Technical Report No. 6, 1956.

Gough, H. G., M. G. McKee, and R. J. Yandell. *Adjective check list analyses of a number of selected psychometric and assessment variables.* Officer Education Research Laboratory, Maxwell Air Force Base, Alabama, Technical Memorandum OERL-TM-55-10, May 1955.

Guilford, J. P. When not to factor-analyze. *Psychological Bulletin,* 1952, 49, 26–37.

———. *Psychometric methods.* New York: McGraw-Hill, 1936.

Gulliksen, H. *Theory of mental tests.* New York: Wiley, 1950.

Guttman, L. The Cornell technique for scale and intensity analysis. *Educational and Psychological Measurement,* 1947, 7, 247–279.

Kelley, T. L. *Activity-preference test for the classification of service personnel.* NDRC, Project SOS-7, OSRD Report No. 4484. Cambridge, Mass.: Harvard University, 1944.

Kriedt, P. H. Vocational interests of psychologists. *Journal of Applied Psychology,* 1949, 33, 482–488.

Kuder, G. F. *Kuder Preference Record, Vocational, Form C.* Chicago: Science Research Associates, 1939, 1951.

————, and M. W. Richardson. The theory of the estimation of test reliability. *Psychometrika*, 1937, 2, 151–160.

Kurz, L. A. A study of the relationship between interest and achievement in air technical training in the Navy. Unpublished master's thesis, Ohio State University, 1951.

Lecznar, W., B. Fruchter, and V. Zachert. *A factor analysis of the airman biographical inventory BE601B*. San Antonio, Texas: Human Resources Research Center, Lackland Air Force Base Research Bulletin, 51-3, March 1951.

Mahalonobis, P. C., D. N. Majundar, and C. R. Rao. Anthropometric survey of the United Provinces, 1941: a statistical survey. *Sankhva*, 1949, 9, 89–324.

Norman, W. T. A spatial analysis of an interest domain. *Educational and Psychological Measurement*, 1960, 20, 347–361.

————. A dispersion analysis of the interests of 115 occupational and reference groups. Unpublished doctoral dissertation, University of Minnesota, 1957.

Perry, D. K. Forced-choice vs. L-I-D response items in vocational interest measurement. Unpublished doctoral dissertation, University of Minnesota, 1953.

Rao, C. R. A note on the distribution of $D^2_{p+q} - D^2_p$ and some computational aspects of the D. statistic and discriminant function. *Sankhva*, 1950, 10, 361–363.

Schenkel, K. F. Tabulator operator selection, emphasizing relationships among aptitudes, interests, proficiency, job- and vocational-satisfaction. Unpublished doctoral dissertation, University of Minnesota, 1953.

Stewart, Naomi. AGCT scores of army personnel grouped by occupation. *Occupations*, 1947, 26, 5–41.

Stogdill, R. M., and K. Koehler. *Measures of leadership structure and organization change*. Columbus: Ohio State University Research Foundation, 1952.

Strong, E. K., Jr. *Strong Vocational Interest Blank*. Palo Alto, Calif.: Consulting Psychologists Press, 1959.

————. *Vocational interests 18 years after college*. Minneapolis: University of Minnesota Press, 1955.

————. *Vocational interests of men and women*. Stanford University, Calif.: Stanford University Press, 1943.

Tatsuoka, M. M., and D. V. Tiedeman. Discriminant analysis. *Revue of Educational Research*, 1954, 24, 402–420.

Thorndike, R. L., and Elizabeth Hagen. 10,000 careers. New York: Wiley, 1959.

Tiedeman, D. V., and J. G. Bryan. Prediction of college field of concentration. *Harvard Educational Revue*, 1954, 24, 122–139.

Tilton, J. W. The measurement of overlapping. *Journal of Educational Psychology*, 1937, 28, 656–662.

Torr, D. V. *A factor analysis of 49 interest variables*. San Antonio, Texas: Human Resources Research Center, Lackland Air Force Base Research Bulletin, 53-67, December 1953.

Triggs, Frances O. A study of the relation of Kuder Preference Record scores to various other measures. *Educational and Psychological Measurement*, 1943, 3, 341–354.

Zuckerman, J. V. A note on "Interest Item Response Arrangement." *Journal of Applied Psychology*, 1953, 37, 94–95.

————. Interest item response arrangement as it affects discrimination between professional groups. *Journal of Applied Psychology*, 1952, 36, 79–85.

Index

Index

standard errors of measurement of, 40–41; use of, 39–40

Occupations, hierarchy of, 53

Overlap: and D, 71–75; percentage of as measure of validity, 22

Perry, D. K.: and items, 18; and job satisfaction, 92

Personality Assessment and Research, Institute for, 56

Psychologists: best scoring key for, 27–28; Strong Vocational Interest Blank and personal descriptions of, 56

Q sorts, and Strong Vocational Interest Blank, 56

Rao, C. R., cluster analysis methods, 97

Radio operators key, homogeneous vs. empirical, 56

Reference groups: civilian, 32; Navy, 33

Reliability: of items, 24–25; of triads, 24–25

Schenkel, K. F., and prediction of proficiency, 90

School achievement, and interests, 83–89

Scoring keys: effects of increasing heterogeneity, 31–38; number of items in, 25–28; plus-one weights only, 51–52; procedures for developing, 37–38; reliability of, 25–26; selection of items for, 30–38; use of weights, 28–30; with small number of items, 48–52

Skilled trades, see Nonprofessional occupations

Standard error of measurement, of empirical keys, 40–41

Stewart, Naomi, and GCT scores for workers, 6, 8

Stogdill, R. M., and roles played by executives, 116

Strong, E. K., Jr.: findings bearing on job satisfaction, 92; follow-up study, 82; objectivity of, 119

Strong Vocational Interest Blank: best key for psychologists, 27–28; correlation of scores with Kuder Preference Record scores, 57–58; item content of, 14; method of scoring, 55; and Q sorts, 56; scores of psychologists and personal descriptions, 56; uses of, 9, 21

Suppressor items in scoring keys, 36–38

Tabulating equipment operators, interests and job performance of, 90–92

Tatsuoka, M. M., and discriminant analysis, 96

Technical occupations, see Nonprofessional occupations

Thorndike, R. L., and occupational classification, 110–112

Tiedeman, D. V., and discriminant analysis, 96, 97

Tilton, J. W., and index of overlap, 22n

Torr, D. V., factor analysis of interest variables, 59

Trade groups: mean scores on Minnesota Vocational Interest Inventory, 45–48; overlapping of interest scores of, 48

Tradesmen in general, as reference groups, 32

Triad, see Item form

Triggs, Frances O., and key correlations, 57

U.S. Employment Service, 90–92

Validity: of homogeneous and empirical keys, 80–81; of occupational keys, 22, 25–38, 44–53

Weights, use in scoring keys, 28–30

Yeomen, job satisfaction and interests, 92–93

Zackert, V., factor analysis of interest variables, 59

Zuckerman, J. V., and item arrangement, 17

129

Date Due

Due	Returned	Due	Returned
Nov. 8 '62	FEB 2 6 1991		
APR 19 1991			